CONCILIUM

Religion in the Seventies

CONCILIUM

Religion in the Seventies

EDITORIAL DIRECTORS:

BASIC EDITORIAL COMMITTEES: Roland Murphy and Bruce Vawter (Scripture) • Giuseppe Alberigo and Anton Weiler (Church History)

EDITORIAL COMMITTEES: *Group I: Christian Faith:* Edward Schillebeeckx and Bas van Iersel (Dogma) • Hans Küng and Walter Kasper (Ecumenism) • Johannes B. Metz and Jean-Pierre Jossua (Fundamental Theology). *Group II: Christian Ethics:* Franz Böckle and Jacques-Marie Pohier (Moral Theology) • Christian Duquoc and Casiano Floristán (Spirituality) • Andrew Greeley and Gregory Baum (Sociology of Religion) *Group III: The Practical Church:* Alois Müller and Norbert Greinacher (Pastoral Theology) • Herman Schmidt and David Power (Liturgy) • Peter Huizing and William Bassett (Canon Law)

THEOLOGICAL ADVISERS: Juan Alfaro • Marie-Dominique Chenu • Yves Congar • Gustavo Gutierrez Merino • René Laurentin • Karl Rahner • Roberto Tucci

LAY SPECIALIST ADVISERS: Luciano Caglioti • August-Wilhelm von Eiff • Paulo Freire • Jean Ladrière • Pedro Lain Entralgo • Paul Ricoeur • Barbara Ward Jackson • Harald Weinrich

EXECUTIVE SECRETARY: (Awaiting new appointment), Arksteestraat 3–5, Nijmegen, The Netherlands

New Series: Volume 2, Number 9. Liturgy

EDITORIAL BOARD: Herman Schmidt • David Power • Mgr Jan van Cauwelaert • Irénée-Henri Dalmais • Luigi Della Torre • Balthasar Fischer • Adalberto Franquesa • Joseph Gelineau • Helmut Hucke • Mgr Denis Hurley • Joseph Jungmann • Aidan Kavanagh • Emil Lengeling • Juan Llopis • Gerard Lukken • Thiery Maertens • Luis Maldonado • Hendrik Manders • Salvatore Marsili • Josef Martín Patino • Juan Mateos • Frederick McManus • Jairo Mejía Gomez • Placid Murray • Franz Nikolasch • Ignacio Oñatibia • Joseph Pascher • Jordi Pinell Pons • Heinrich Rennings • Juan Rivera Recio • Philippe Rouillard • Alfredo Trusso • Cipriano Vagaggini • Cyrille Vogel • Mgr Guilford Young

LITURGICAL EXPERIENCE
OF FAITH

Edited by

Herman Schmidt and
David Power

Herder and Herder

1973
HERDER AND HERDER NEW YORK
815 Second Avenue
New York 10017

ISBN: 0-8164-2538-8

Cum approbatione Ecclesiastica

Library of Congress Catalog Card Number: 72-12420

Printed in the United States

CONTENTS

Editorial

THE Church's liturgy is both a continuation of and a participation in the worship of the Father by Christ, the Son of God and the head of the human race. Firstly, he is the Son of the Father and he expresses this for us in a sacramental way in the liturgy. Secondly, the liturgy also communicates grace to us, making us sons of God. As members of the Church, we participate in Christ's liturgy. The Church's liturgical participation in Christ's sonship makes our sonship of God visible and active. Our faith as sons of God is most completely expressed and most intensely experienced in the liturgy, and faith, together with hope, love and conversion, is the soul of the liturgy and its content.[1]

How is this faith expressed and experienced by the Christian community in the liturgy? The authors of the contributions to this number attempt to answer this question from different points of view. The first, Gerard Lukken, describes the liturgical community's unique, intimate and personal expression of faith in the Father, the Son and the Holy Spirit. The second author, Bruce Vawter, outlines the growth of this liturgical expression of faith in the New Testament, and the third, Evangelista Vilanova, its growth in the early post-apostolic churches.

A detailed analysis of the language of faith in the liturgical community provided in the next three articles forms the core of this number. Jean-Pierre Manigne discusses this language as

[1] See the article on faith ("*Geloof*") in *Liturgisch Woordenboek* (Roermond and Maaseik, 1958–1962), pp. 819–26.

7

poetic language, Jean Ladrière as performative language and Langdon Gilkey as the language of God to man and of man to God. The reader must be prepared for technical terminology in these articles, but he should not be deterred because these authors write very clearly and define their terms very precisely.

The last articles deal at greater depth with a number of important aspects of the liturgy. Firstly, the influence of the social environment on the liturgical expression and experience of faith in the Christian community is discussed with reference to the striking example of the Syro–Palestinian rite by I.-H. Dalmais. Secondly, Casper Honders shows how the confession of faith has always been and still must be accompanied by a confession of sin. Thirdly, David Power points to the difference between the language games of the liturgy and of theology.

Finally, Mariasusai Dhavamony discusses the possible contribution of Hinduism to the Christian liturgy in a bulletin. We were unfortunately not able to obtain a bulletin on Buddhism, but preferred to leave a gap rather than provide something which would simply fill in space. A documentation on faith and its confession in an a-religious world (Herman Schmidt) concludes this number of *Concilium*.

HERMAN SCHMIDT
DAVID POWER

PART I
ARTICLES

Gerard Lukken

The Unique Expression of Faith in the Liturgy

I. A CRUCIAL PROBLEM

DESPITE the emphasis placed in distinctively human experience nowadays, this experience has in practice been severely reduced and modern man, his feelings obstructed and his perception clouded, is no longer able to experience reality freely. His body and senses play a minor part in his understanding of reality. Fortmann called this the crucial problem of Western civilization [1] and pointed out that man's increasing disincarnation has led to disturbances in his emotional life and an impoverishment in his perceptive powers. He perceives reality, Fortmann maintained, in the light of a rational system of concepts inherited from the past and inserted into the future.[2] In Fortmann's opinion, this is not only a social, but also a religious problem, because man cannot encounter God unless his experience of reality is unclouded.[3] This disincarnation of man in Western society has had a very profound effect on the Christian churches. As a direct result, they have tended to overemphasize moral and religious teaching as opposed to human feeling and sensory perception, which they have come to distrust. In recent years, this tendency seems even to have increased, orthodox teaching being emotionally defended in passionate theological argument. Those Christians who have tried to give form to the social context of Christian faith have

[1] H. Fortmann, *Wat is er met de mens gebeurd?* (Bilthoven, 1971); *idem, Oosterse Renaissance* (Bilthoven, 1970), pp. 9–18.
[2] Fortmann, *Oosterse Renaissance, op. cit.*, pp. 13–14.   [3] *Ibid.*

found themselves obliged to accord central importance to questions of truth and this has compromised the Christian's full experience of faith.

II. Kerygma as a Call to Faith

Scripture emphasizes the dynamic aspects of the Word as an event and the kerygma is the proclamation of Christ's work of salvation which is directed towards man's encounter with God. Calling on the listener to give himself in faith to the God of salvation, the kerygma is both the proclamation and the bringing about of salvation and therefore much more than simply a making of theological or dogmatic statements. It is even more true than theology or dogma, because in it truth is an event which takes place in man.[4] Although it is firmly based in tradition, it must therefore also speak directly to the whole man in his contemporary social context, taking account of his personal feelings and his human experience. "In season and out of season" (2 Tim. 4. 2), the kerygma must be proclaimed in such a way that it provides an original answer to the questions asked by man here and now.[5]

If Fortmann's contention that the impoverishment of man's perceptive powers is a crucial social and religious problem of our times is correct, then the kerygma will inevitably fail as long as it is limited to a call to accept truths. It must, as Fortmann insisted, above all be a call to the whole man to "rediscover God as the answer to *all* questions and as the creator of *all* things" and to turn towards Christ as the light of the world with all his powers.[6] Its aim is to persuade man to accept in faith that God is his redeemer in this world and in this history and through Christ and that this faith is not a doctrine, but in a person.

This kerygma makes an appeal not only to the whole man who hears it, but also to the one who proclaims it. There are, in fact, not two parties, one speaking and the other listening, but a tentative seeking together for a common faith. The kerygma returns

---

[4] *Handboek van de Pastoraaltheologie* (Hilversum, 1966–1968), II, pp. 35–38; III, pp. 110–19.
[5] W. Bless, "What are the Main Requirements for a New Catechism?", *Concilium*, March 1970 (American Edn., Vol. 53).
[6] H. Fortmann, *Als ziende de Onzienlijke* (Hilversum, 1964), I, p. 304.

to the one who proclaims it as an appeal.[7] Even though it is the Lord himself whose Spirit is active when the kerygma is proclaimed, it makes a considerable difference if the one who proclaims it really experiences the kerygma with the whole of his being. If this is not the case, the result will be confusion rather than salvation, because the one proclaiming the kerygma will unconsciously use it as a cover for his own problems and this will lead to a blockage in communication between him and those who hear it, so that the kerygma may become a purely negative framework.[8]

III. FAITH IS EXPRESSED IN AND THROUGH THE LITURGY

The kerygma leads man to an existential decision concerning faith, to cease to be inert and to give himself to the event proclaimed. In other words, he moves from *metanoia* to self-abandonment. This deep inward experience is, however, not fully faith—it only becomes authentically human when man gives it form. Faith must be expressed and it is only through this expression that man can participate in the saving event towards which his faith is directed. In this, Christian behaviour is less important as an expression of faith than the words and symbols of the liturgy which concern the whole man and bring about a true communication between God and man and his fellow men.[9]

The pre-conciliar theology of the Church tended to teach that the liturgy expressed a faith which was already present and was a condition for full participation in the liturgical act, which in turn confirmed that faith. Now, however, we see faith as more than a condition and the liturgy as more than a confirmation— faith is above all expressed in the words and symbols of the liturgy.[10] Liturgical expression is therefore an essential aspect of faith, causing it to become an "act".

[7] W. Bless, *op. cit.*; A. Bosse, "Wat vereist verkondiging?", *Ons Gesstelijk Leven*, 49 (1972), pp. 71–80.

[8] J. Piper, "Klinische Seelsorge-Ausbildung", *Berliner Hefte für evangelische Krankenseelsorge*, 30 (1972), pp. 30–44.

[9] A. Vergote, "Expressie als ervaring en als handeling", *Tijdschrift voor Theologie*, 56 (1972), pp. 15–28.

[10] H. Manders, "The Meaning of Faith in Adult Baptism", *Concilium*, Feb. 1967 (American Edn., Vol. 22); A. Vergote, "Symbolic Gestures and Actions in the Liturgy", *Concilium*, Feb. 1971 (American Edn., Vol. 62).

One question that inevitably arises in this context is, however, how can the liturgy be an act of *God* so long as it is characterized as an expression of *human* faith? But surely there can never be competition between God and man? Surely God reveals and communicates himself to man through human acts? And surely man is turned, by the liturgical expression of faith, towards the saving event of Jesus? The God of salvation is actively present only when man expresses his faith liturgically. In the liturgy, the whole man turns towards God (trans-as-cendence) and God happens to man as the gift which redeems him (trans-des-cendence). Liturgy is therefore communication between God and man and between man and God, God taking the initiative. There is an active element (the symbol as man's expression) and a passive element (the same symbol as God's expression) in the liturgy.

Baptism provides a good example of this liturgical expression of faith. Firstly, the confession of faith both expresses the faith of the candidate and of the Christian community and is the symbol (*symbolum*) in and through which the event of baptism is revealed and given by God to the candidate. Then the candidate is immersed in water—the immersion is performed by the Christian community as an act in Jesus' name, so that it is the Lord himself who baptizes the candidate. In the confession of faith, the accent falls on the active part played by the believer; in the immersion, the accent falls on the passive part played by the believer.

Faith, then, is more than a condition for the liturgy and the liturgy is more than a confirmation of faith—each is an integral part of the other and *ex opere operato* and *ex opere operantis* are integral aspects of the liturgy itself. What are the consequences of this? A contrast is sometimes drawn between an objective and a subjective liturgy, the latter stemming from the believer's personal experience. This contrast is, however, without foundation, because the same liturgy which expresses God's salvation at the same time expresses man's faith and the liturgy fails essentially if it does not express that faith. It must not lead to alienation. It must address the whole man—his intellect, his emotions, his body and his senses. If the liturgy is not experienced as a living reality, there may be faith in the community, but it will not become an "act" and there will be no full and mature encounter between man and God.

IV. Conversion and Praise as Aspects of the Expression of Faith

1. *Conversion*

The kerygma calls man to conversion. This is an essential aspect of faith, a radical process which lasts the whole of the believer's life. Even though the fundamental characteristics of *metanoia* remain the same, each believer and each generation of believers must experience it differently. In the modern world, for example, man's macrosphere must be taken into account in considering *metanoia*.[11] Evil has increased greatly in scale and man has to be converted from this. True conversion to the God of salvation, who entered the history of man in the person of Jesus and fulfils it through his Spirit, can only take place nowadays when man is converted in this way.

This *metanoia* must also be expressed before it can take place and here too Christian behaviour is less important as an expression than the words and symbols of the liturgy which concern the whole man and his conversion. This symbolism is essential if conversion is to be fully experienced and this conversion is also essential to the liturgy as such.

However important it may be for man to be converted from his individual sins, it is even more important nowadays to look for liturgical forms of expression of consciousness of sin and of *metanoia* in the macrosphere. (In this context, political and cosmo-political elements in the liturgy, however unbalanced they may at times be, are vitally important in an authentic expression of *metanoia*.) Conversion has always been expressed in the Church's liturgy. Again, baptism provides us with a good example of the candidate's turning away from the West and spitting at the kingdom of Satan. The works of the devil which he abjured in this way were visible and concrete in the worship of idols and in the pagan world as a whole. In the *Didascalia*, the bishop was urged to give up his *cathedra* to the poor man who

[11] See *Concilium*, Jan. 1971 (American Edn., Vol. 61).

joined the community.[12] In the same way, liturgical form must be given to *metanoia* in our modern society if it is to become an "act".

The liturgy expresses this *metanoia* in word and symbol and brings about a reconciliation between God and the community—not simply the individual—in its macro-dimensions. This communal aspect of conversion is sometimes overemphasized in contemporary liturgy, expressing a desire to change the world and to banish pain and suffering, but this may be because the theology of the Cross has been excluded by the theology of the healthy.[13] The believer must, of course, turn away from evil in the world, but only the Cross can save him from this evil. The suffering servant of Yahweh was the victim of the powers of darkness during his life, but these powers were conquered and reconciliation was achieved in his death. The man who is converted can only boast of the Cross.

2. *Praise*

Although praise is undoubtedly the climax of the liturgical expression of faith, the contemporary Christian apparently finds it difficult to express this element, partly perhaps because of the impoverishment of his perceptive powers of which Fortmann spoke. It cannot be disputed that real praise can only be given by the whole man who is fully and deeply involved in the world with all his emotions and senses and is therefore to some extent primitive and possessed by a sense of wonder and admiration. It is only if he is converted to a primary experience of reality that the believer can discover for himself the wonder of creation and praise God for it. The whole man is set in motion in this praise, which is spontaneously expressed in song and dance as well as in words.

However important the noetic aspect of praise may be, it is never of primary importance. The same also applies to the liturgical confession of faith, which originated in the early Church as a hymn or doxology—a praise (*logos*) of God's glory (*doxa*). The emphasis was not on the doctrinal content in the early Church.

[12] A. Hamman, *Vie liturgique et vie sociale* (Paris, 1968), p. 297.
[13] J. Ratzinger, "Einheit der Kirche—Einheit der Menschheit", *Internationale Katholische Zeitschrift*, 1 (1972), p. 81,

Gradually, however, the emphasis changed and, from the time of the Council of Chalcedon onwards, the confession of faith became less and less a liturgical doxology and more and more a formulation of doctrine, a development which reached its peak in the Tridentine confession of faith (Denz. 1862, 1870) and has been continued in, for example, the more recent anti-modernist oath (Denz. 3537–3550) and in Paul VI's *Professio Fidei* of 1968. Fortunately, there has been a growing tendency in the last few years to evolve confessions of faith in which praise forms an essential element.[14]

Another reason why the contemporary Christian finds it difficult to express his faith in praise is because he is so conscious of evil in the macrosphere. "How shall we sing the Lord's song in a foreign land?" the psalmist asked (Ps. 137. 4). How can modern man dance and sing when people are being tortured in Brazil? How can we praise the Lord when the whole of creation is groaning?[15]

It is, I believe, possible for us to proclaim God's praise, but only after we have experienced *metanoia* in the sense outlined above, that is, after we have inwardly experienced Jesus' suffering and death on the Cross as a conquest of the powers of evil. Through our experience of the Cross in the liturgy, we can be reconciled and go on to life, praise, song and dance, even in circumstances which are very painful. The Christian who reaches the stage where he can experience and express his faith in this way will know that death, which is constantly threatened by the powers of evil, is not what men imagine it to be. He who has died lives. In other words, the powerful are really weak, the last will be first, the loser wins and the lost one will be saved. Strengthened by this Easter praise, the Christian can experience the sufferings of the world as his own.[16]

[14] For confessions of faith generally, see *Concilium*, Jan. 1970 (American Edn., Vol. 51); see also A. Brekelmans, "Origin and Function of Creeds in the Early Church", *Concilium*, Jan. 1970 (American Edn., Vol. 51); J. Lescrauwaet, "Confessing the Faith in the Liturgy", *Concilium*, April 1970 (American Edn., Vol. 54); E. Schlink, "Die Strukturen der dogmatischen Aussage als oekumenisches Problem", *Kerygma und Dogma*, 3 (1957), pp. 265 ff.

[15] J. Moltmann, *Het spel van de vrijheid* (Bilthoven, 1971), pp. 9–10.

[16] J. Moltmann, *op. cit.*, pp. 29–37.

V. The Church and Man's Expression of Faith

Faith is above all expressed communally by the people of God. The man who confesses his faith and accepts baptism not only expresses that faith as an individual, but also enters the community of the universal Church and joins in its expression of faith. But this universal Church finds its concrete experience in the local community, which inevitably bears the features of the social environment in which it is situated. This means that there will be pluriformity in the expression of faith. Because there are so many social, educational, economic and other differences even within the same geographical region, faith may be expressed very differently even within the liturgy of the local church.

This has, for many reasons, resulted in serious tensions in the Church. Many Catholic Christians are, for example, still ignorant of the emphasis placed in recent ecclesiology on the local community. They still see the Church as a centralized structure with all authority invested in Rome and all liturgical expression of faith as a uniform and official "state art" of the "perfect society" of the Church.[17] In that Church, the local community could contribute nothing to the liturgy and had the task simply of carrying out the prescribed universal liturgy. This of course led to the living faith of the people becoming alienated from the official liturgy of the Church, to a striking contrast between the subjective expression of the people's faith and the so-called objective liturgy. The inevitable result of this was the emergence at the local level of paraliturgical practices which ought, strictly speaking, to be called original local liturgical practices. This alienation or contrast can only be overcome by giving much more emphasis, in the spirit of Vatican II, to the local community,[18] not only the bishops' conferences, but also the local church, monastic community, Christian meeting and even family or house group, within which faith can be expressed in a unique liturgical manner.

[17] J. Peters, "The Many Forms of the One Prayer", *Concilium*, Feb. 1970 (American Edn., Vol. 52).

[18] *Liturgische Oriëntatie na Vaticanum II*, Supplement to *Liturgisch Woordenboek* (Roermond, 1970), pp. 13-17, 20-21; H. Reifenberg, "Die Liturgiewissenschaft und die Liturgie der Teilkirchen", in *Archiv für Liturgiewissenschaft*, 11 (1969), pp. 179-81, 208-13.

Clearly, the existing liturgy cannot be preserved simply for its own sake. In the tradition of the Church, the living expression of faith has always taken many forms and this pluriformity need not be seen now as a threat to the unity and universality of the Church. This unity will be guaranteed so long as the responsibility of the office of the bishop and the priest is revalued. The priest must safeguard the universal openness of the liturgy in his parish community to the liturgy in other parish structures. The bishop must ensure that the liturgy in his diocese is open to that of other dioceses and the Church province must do the same with regard to other provinces, with Rome at the centre. At this centre of the Church, it is necessary to provide a framework of basic liturgical structures which fully respect the contribution made by the local community.

If this ideal is realized, the Church will no longer be experienced as something placed between God and man or as a cause of alienation. After all, the family structure is not placed between parents and children, because it is formed by their life together. The Church is the presence of the Lord only in so far as he is visibly present in the concrete assembly of the local communities which are inwardly united under the successor of Peter. If this concrete assembly of the local communities is respected in the liturgical expression of faith, the Church will no longer be experienced as a roundabout way to encounter God.[19]

VI. THE LITURGY AS "THEOLOGIA" AND "ORTHODOXIA PRIMA"

In the early Church and especially in the East, the liturgy was known as *theologia prima* and dogmatic speculation as *theologia secunda*. The first meaning of "orthodoxy" was also right praise (*ortho-doxia*) in the liturgy and it is only in the secondary, derived sense that it came to mean right teaching.[20] It is therefore quite legitimate to speak of an *orthodoxia prima* and an *orthodoxia secunda*.

[19] See *Handbuch der Pastoraltheologie* (Freiburg i. Br., 1964–66), II.
[20] E. Griese, "Perspektiven einer liturgischen Theologie", in *Una Sancta*, 24 (1969), pp. 102 ff.; W. Kasper, *Dogma unter dem Wort Gottes* (Mainz, 1965), p. 33; L. Lescrauwaet, *op. cit.*; R. Stahlin, "Die Geschichte des christlichen Gottesdienstes", in *Leitourgia-Handbuch des evangelischen Gottesdienstes* (Kassel, 1954), I, p. 29.

The phrases *theologia* and *orthodoxia prima*, then, point to the liturgy in which faith is expressed and as such the liturgy is the first source and the norm from which teaching is derived. Faith is expressed in the most original, reliable and compelling way in the liturgy. God gives himself completely to man and man abandons himself to God in Jesus and through the Holy Spirit in the liturgical complex of words and symbols. This liturgical expression of faith is much richer than any intellectual expression or justification of faith in theological argument or dogmatic pronouncement because of this radical encounter which can only take place in this way in the liturgy and nowhere else. Theological speculation ought therefore to be nourished by the liturgical expression of faith, but it is undoubtedly true to say that theology and liturgy have become increasingly alienated from each other, especially since the Council of Trent.[21]

In the same way, orthodoxy, in the second and later sense of right teaching, became predominant in the Church and it was not until the Second Vatican Council that the balance was redressed and emphasis was once again given to the idea of orthodoxy as the liturgical expression of faith. Yet, although it is within the authentic tradition of the Church to give priority to this *orthodoxia prima*, this living liturgy has constantly to be subject to the criticism of the *theologia* and *orthodoxia secunda*, without which the Spirit is always in danger of being extinguished in the liturgy. A relationship of constant dialogue between *theologia* and *orthodoxia prima* and *secunda* is essential if we are to ensure that the liturgy does not once again become isolated from the living faith of the Church.[22]

VII. Conclusion

In the midst of the heated theological discussions and the struggle to reassert the *orthodoxia secunda*, will the Church find the courage to be converted to the primacy of the *theologia* and

---

[21] C. Vagaggini, *Il senso teologico della liturgia* (Rome, 2nd edn., 1958), pp. 416–29.
[22] D. von Allmen, "Das Problem einer 'einheimischen' Theologie im Lichte des Neuen Testaments", *Evangelische Missions-Zeitschrift*, 27 (1970), pp. 57–71, 160–75.

orthodoxia prima? A conversion to authentic liturgical practice might, after all, be the right way of bringing and keeping Christians together in *one* Church. The *communio* of all believers with the one Lord and with each other is experienced and expressed in a unique way in the liturgy and we should not underestimate the ecumenical significance of this.

Translated by David Smith

The Development of the Expression of Faith in the Worshipping Community

(a) *In the New Testament*

Bruce Vawter

IT WAS Eduard Norden who some sixty years ago forged the form-critical tools that are now used to uncover the liturgical-hymnic source-materials redacted into the New Testament.[1] Neither liturgical influence on the New Testament nor the presence of hymns there was an original discovery by Norden, of course. Besides the obvious and explicit references to liturgy in Acts and the Epistles, and the many Gospel passages which have been shaped to allow for liturgical allusions, there has hardly ever been any serious doubt that—to take one example—the "Jesus is Lord" formula of Rom. 10. 9 and 1 Cor. 12. 3 was lifted by Paul straight from the liturgical experience of the Christian communities of Rome and Corinth. As for hymns, those of Luke and Revelation were always recognized as classic. What form criticism did was to bring the two together, liturgy and hymn, or rather, make it possible for us to see how the two had conspired together to make up one of the earliest Christian theologies, whose destiny it was to help create and at the same time be absorbed by the New Testament canon.

The hymns which appear explicitly and integrally in the New Testament books may or may not have been original compositions by their canonical authors and may or may not have been liturgically influenced in their beginning as they were later in their use: the evidence is fairly evenly divided in either direction.

[1] *Agnostos Theos: Untersuchungen zur Formengeschichte religiöser Rede* (Leipzig and Berlin, 1913).

The Lucan canticles, which serve a diagrammatic function iden-
tical with that of the sermons of Acts, are substantive to the
structure of the Third Gospel, the work of a consummate artist
who has so made them his own that their pre-canonical character,
if any, can only be guessed at and hardly proved.[2] Something very
similar must be said of the hymns of Revelation, which badly
need a thorough form-critical study. In these "heavenly liturgies" we find doxologies, acclamations of acceptance (*Würdig-
Rufe*) and other forms of a cultic flavour which show the author
to have been at home with liturgical thought, but they cannot
be certainly related to any existing practice of the Church.[3] The
hymns, or hymnic fragments, of which form criticism has ap-
prised us, are rather those which the canonical authors found
already to hand in the credal and liturgical life of their churches,
which therefore affected their theology in the very act of being
modified or revised by redactional use. Norden's criteria for the
isolation of these passages, aside from their evident poetic character and pecularities of vocabulary, were principally their high
incidence of participles and relative clauses,[4] traits that suited
them admirably to be the expansions of prayers of blessing or
thanksgiving. To be sure, he did not then know all the con-
clusions that would ultimately be drawn from his insights; his
criteria had to be sharpened by another long generation of literary
study. Nevertheless, he deserves full credit for our being able
today to point with modest certainty to the remains of a respect-
able corpus of early Christian hymnody imbedded mainly in the
epistolary of the New Testament which may very well put us in
touch with some of the first language uttered by the Church in
its christological prayer.

The passages with which we are concerned, if we restrict the
list to those that are beyond debate (most of which were identified
by Norden), are Phil. 2, 6–11, Col. 1. (12–14), 15–20 + 2. 10; Eph.

---

[2] See the discussions of P. Minear, C. F. D. Moule, E. Schweizer, among
others, in *Studies in Luke-Acts* (Paul Schubert Festschrift) (Nashville and
New York, 1966).

[3] Cf. Gerhard Delling, "Zum gottesdienstlichen Stil der Johannes-
Apokalypse", *Novum Testamentum*, 3 (1959), pp. 107–37. On the role
of the doxologies in the structure of Rev., see Ugo Vanni, *La struttura
letteraria dell'Apocalisse* (Rome, 1971), pp. 149–67.

[4] *Op. cit.*, pp. 166–76, 254–63, 380–87.

2. 14–16, 5. 14+(?); 1 Tim. 3. 16; Heb. 1. 3; 1 Pet. 3. 18–22; John 1. 1–5 + 9–11. All of them, with the exception of the Johannine hymn, have the literary characteristics we have just mentioned. For most of them the term "homology" has been found appropriate: that is, as distinct from the "creed" which proclaimed to the world as objects of faith the saving acts of God, these were acclamations in the Church of the Lord in whom salvation had been accomplished. The distinction is a useful one but must not be pressed. Obviously it was for their credal values that Paul and the other New Testament authors saw fit to incorporate such acclamations into their works; and it is for those values that we now deal with them.

What kind of christology was presupposed in these confessions? We might offer the following as elements of a composite,[5] presuming that even though all do not occur in any single example, they are sometimes implied there, and their recurrence is well enough distributed to postulate one doctrine rather than random and discrete pieties (remembering, too, that our examples are fragmentary at best)

1. The Redeemer is united with or equal to God (Phil., Col., Heb., John).
2. He is mediator or an agent in creation (Col., John).
3. He sustains creation (Col., Heb., John).
4. He descends from the heavenly to the earthly realm (Phil., John).
5. He dies (Phil., Col., 1 Tim., 1 Pet.).
6. He is made alive again (Col., 1 Tim., 1 Pet.).
7. He is reconciler (Col., Eph., 1 Tim., 1 Pet., Heb.).
8. He is exalted, enthroned, over the cosmic powers (Phil., 1 Tim., 1 Pet., Heb.).

It is not sufficient, however, merely to note the elements; they must also be evaluated. The death of the Redeemer, for example, in this christology is not the equivalent of the Pauline doctrine of the Cross. It has been adjusted to that doctrine only by evident redactional additions in the Phil. and Col. pericopes. For the rest, it remains a fairly statistical rather than a salutary event:

[5] We use here the eightfold division of J. T. Sanders, *The New Testament Christological Hymns* (Cambridge, 1971), pp. 24–5. He does not include Col. 2. 10 or Eph. 5. 14 in his inventory.

it was destined, it happened, it was a *sine qua non*, the inevitable outcome of life in the flesh, the culmination of a self-abasement and subjection to the action of the powers of the world. We have an echo, then, of the primitive kerygma as it is represented in the first chapters of Acts, in which the crucifixion was largely a negative event cancelled out by the vindication of the resurrection. In these hymns, however, the resurrection itself, though central and all-informing in its effects, does not appear in explicit detail. Rather, what is featured is the exalted state of the Redeemer, his life of the spirit in which he effects salvation here and now, having achieved a cosmic reconciliation. The resurrection is not a vindication, but, at the most, the implied means that led to a vindication; vindication, as matter of fact, is less what is meant by this exaltation than simply another sphere of existence in a divine economy. It goes without saying, of course, that the resurrection does not figure, as it does for Paul, as the ground and exemplar of the Christian's eschatological hope. The eschatology of these hymns is "realized".

Even in Eph. 5. 14, which some believe to have been part of the hymn continued in 1. Tim. 3. 16, and in which alone there is mention of a resurrection—of the believer, not of Christ—the exhortation is to a present, not a future awakening. The *epiphausko* of this verse is *hapax legomenon* in the New Testament, but the idea of "illumination" as well as its other content strongly indicates a baptismal liturgy as a likely setting for the composition. Paul, for whom "light" is a term for the present reality of the Christian life (Rom. 13. 12, 2 Cor. 4. 6, 6. 14, 1 Thes. 5. 5), while always retaining his eschatological perspective on salvation, nevertheless in his sacramental references is very mindful of proleptic realization: "alive to God" (Rom. 6. 11), "eats and drinks judgment" (1 Cor. 11. 29). Indeed, we may ask whether we should not expect those theological utterances which originated in the liturgy, with its twin concern to "presentify" past event and future fulfilment, to have been a wellspring of realized eschatology here and elsewhere in the New Testament.[6] This supposition may be the more readily enter-

---

[6] The thesis of D. E. Aune, *The Cultic Setting of Realized Eschatology in Early Christianity*. Supplement to *Novum Testamentum*, 28 (Leyden, 1972).

tained when we recognize, as most seem to do these days, that there was no necessary descent of realized out of final eschatology, even though this development did take place, but that the former could coexist with the latter and be of equal antiquity with it. (By the same token, it is not required of us to go along with more recent hypotheses such as that of John A. T. Robinson, according to whom the dominant eschatology of early Christianity was an apocalypticized version of one that with Jesus had been originally "realized".) Another factor that must be taken into account is the genius of Christianity itself working instinctively in its liturgy as the faith and thanksgiving response to the saving acts of God. The genius of Christianity is that of a cosmic event which has altered the course of the world with consequent impact on its own awareness of its universal Saviour.[7]

If there has been general agreement concerning the liturgical provenance of these hymns, however, there is also a singular reluctance on the part of most scholars to venture opinions about what precise kind of liturgy it was.[8] For practically any one of the examples with which we have been dealing equally plausible settings have been suggested in both the baptismal and the eucharistic rituals of the first Christian communities. This ambiguity must also be taken into account as part of the phenomenology of these hymns. What it indicates is a mould of thought and language predating the liturgies in which the hymns served, a mould that has shaped both their pre-canonical christology and also the language of the liturgy.

There seems to be no doubt that the moulding influence we are seeking was a wisdom tradition of some sort. Not unnaturally, the wisdom tradition of the Old Testament, including its development in the Alexandrian Judaism represented in the Wisdom of Solomon, has been ransacked for its store of words and themes in order to account for the intellectual climate in which this kind of Christian thinking took form. Some scholars cling to the view that one need look no further than the Old Testament, but such a position is increasingly difficult to defend.

[7] Cf. Reinhard Deichgräber, *Gotteshymnus und Christushymnus in der frühen Christenheit* (Göttingen, 1967), pp. 208–14. He dates all the hymns in the Hellenistic period of the Church.

[8] *Ibid.*, pp. 131–3, 137, 140, 154–5.

"Image of God", "firstborn of every creature", the hypostasis of creative wisdom, and so on, can certainly be derived from the Old Testament tradition, but probably not in exactly the form they achieved in the New Testament. Intertestamental studies have rendered old-fashioned any concept of a monolithic Judaism single-mindedly devoted to the Old Testament as the matrix from which the nascent Church emerged. For the same reason it is unnecessary to follow Rudolf Bultmann's lead, as many do, in seeking a non-Jewish or off-beat Jewish[9] origin of this christology in an equally closed off world of gnostic or pre-gnostic thought. Some of it does correspond with this thought: "head of the body", "flesh and spirit", *Logos*, the inimical powers, etc., while the closest parallels so far found for Eph. 2. 14 occur in the Hermetic and Mandean literatures. But it also contains much that is quite incompatible with a gnostic point of view, including its most basic assertions which are of far greater consequence than any amount of linguistic similarities. We feel that the best evidence still favours a composition of these hymns in light of the Christ-event, not a Christian adaptation of a previously existing redemptive theology; but the composition took place within the complex of speculation and catch-words which passed for philosophy in a syncretistic age, which liturgy found peculiarly adaptable to its needs.

It seems to be entirely appropriate that the earliest language of liturgy should have been ready-made and not its own creation. If *lex orandi lex credendi* is a genuine principle—if the liturgy gives expression to a faith held by the community and is not, as is often the case nowadays, the attempt to form a faith by changing the terms of liturgy—then the language which liturgy chose must have already existed as one option among others and was plastic to uses other than the liturgical. It is also entirely appropriate that the choice should have descended on the language of wisdom. The participles and relatives which for the most part characterize the first Christian liturgy were acts of blessings or thanksgiving appended to acclamations of the Church's Lord. It was in wisdom circles, before and after the coming of Christianity (as we know from the Odes of Solomon, for example), that

[9] The conclusion ultimately reached by Sanders.

the thanksgiving hymn found a particular repository; and it was the same circles that were the most hospitable to speculation in those spheres where worship celebrated its thanks for God's saving activity: nature, creation, man, the cosmos.

At the same time, it is surely not without significance that probably in no single instance does any one of the liturgical hymns of which we have been speaking appear now in the New Testament in the exact language in which it was first composed. The redactional changes introduced by the canonical authors extend in almost every instance not merely to editorial adjustments demanded by new contexts but also to the actual substance of the material. Is this phenomenon related to the inadequacy of language taken in the whole, the principle that "speech is bounded by silence",[10] that theological formulations in each successive stage require further translation and rearticulation? Or is it an indication of the inherent inadequacy of the theology caught up by the hymns, of its unsuitability for kerygmatic proclamation? Of Phil. 2. 6–11 Hans Conzelmann has said, "no gospel could be written in the light of this christology", because of its minimization of history and susceptibility to myth.[11] Probably we should answer both of these questions affirmatively.

The theology of the hymns was not only adapted by the New Testament authors but also changed. In Phil. 2. 8 "death on a cross" may perhaps be considered a minor amplification, but "of the church" in Col. 1. 18 certainly is not. At the same time, what took place in redaction should not be exaggerated into a correction of heterodoxy. Had this been the situation, we should doubtless never have had the hymns preserved for us in the first place: they were preserved because of the respect accorded them, even though it was a critical respect.[12] The christology they professed was not timeless and unhistorical, though it dealt with a minimum number of events selectively. What accounts for the discrepancies between the pre-canonical and the canonical texts are mainly the separate requirements of prayer on the one hand and credal articu-

[10] Sanders, op. cit., pp. 140–41; cf. also Deichgräber, op. cit., p. 206.
[11] An Outline of the Theology of the New Testament (New York, 1969), p. 80.
[12] As the present author has argued in "The Colossians Hymn and the Principle of Redaction", Catholic Biblical Quarterly (1971), pp. 62–81.

lation on the other. Externally, too, there was an undeniable pressure in the Pauline churches in favour of the more "standard" theological expression to which they had become accustomed, coupled, no doubt, with a growing suspicion against wisdom formulations because of their greater openness to gnostic and docetic thought.

The liturgical experience of early Christianity, as seen in the development of the christological hymns and their subsequent literary history, was unique, and it might be perilous to extrapolate from it to later liturgical experiences which may in part resemble it. We can only recapitulate the stages of the experience for what they show to have been New Testament convictions. It adapted rather than attempted to formulate anew the language in which it chose to express itself, falling back upon concepts which it found most congenial to its needs and tastes, some of which were especially congruent with the liturgical life-setting. The existential rather than the eschatological aspect of that setting was favoured, whether by design or natural affinity. The derivation of its speech, together with its easy redaction before and after its incorporation into the canonical texts, encourage us at least to recognize that on this precedent it is not language itself that is sacred but only what is done with language.

(b) *In the Post-Apostolic Age*

Evangelista Vilanova

BECAUSE a full-scale study would be impossible here, I confine myself to the interpretation of two crucial formulations of the faith of the primitive community, in the sacraments of baptism and the Eucharist. I mean the creed and the anaphora or canon. These two formulae do not of course contain the whole of the sacraments but they are pre-eminently important in the study of the relationship between faith and worship and have therefore been the subject of much historical and textual research.

In the earliest tradition baptism and Eucharist appear as sacraments of faith: the Eucharist confesses in praise and thanksgiving that same faith proclaimed in baptism. The history of the liturgy shows us how closely the baptismal catechesis issuing in the creed corresponds with the themes of the eucharistic prayer.[1]

I. From the Beginning to the Composition of the Creed

The need for faithfulness to the teaching of the apostles resulted, in the primitive Church, in the creation of baptismal creeds, either in the form of question and answer or of a recited confession of faith. And we know that originally the word creed did not mean only the baptismal confession of faith. For Latin Christians it had a broader reference, suggested by its Greek etymology; it was, it seems, a "sign of recognition". The *symbolum* is the visible face of the mystery of God. The structure itself of the faith is conditioned by its formulation. For this faith is not a jealously guarded secret. It must be communicated in order to become the common bond of the fraternal community; because the characteristic of the Christian faith is to be received and lived in the Church, it must be translated into communicable formulae, signs of recognition and unity in Christ.

However, it must be said that the text of the creed emerges from a strictly liturgical linguistic situation. It is a confession of faith proclaimed within a believing community. Its language is clearly defined and has developed slowly, a process which required *belief*. Although its semantic context is largely biblical (which was why there was such a fuss about the *homoousios* innovation), it is also precisely theological and christological in tone.

Although at this period liturgical formulae had great flexibility, the text known since the fourth century as the "Apostles' Creed" is the result of a long process of development and, according to historians, a combination of two confessions, one trinitarian and the other christological, the latter being added to the former. It is no surprise that the creed as an act of faith is primarily an invocation and only secondly a theological statement.

[1] A. Hamman, "Du symbole de la foi à l'anaphore eucharistique", *Kyriakon. Festschrift J. Quasten*, vol. ii (Münster, 1970), pp. 835-43.

Perhaps it would be better to say that the theological language of the creed is christological. For indeed "Jesus is Lord" is the central Christian belief. But St Paul himself confessing that "Jesus is Lord" believed in God before he believed that Jesus was the Lord and Jesus refers to God his Father, God the Creator.

The Apostles' Creed is an austere confession of faith. It remains quite simple, secure in the faith of the community. It was naturally invoked in disputes with heretics. But this was putting the creed to a use for which it was not primarily intended; it was taken word for word as a means of defending the purity of faith. It is often said that the Council of Nicaea took the faith received in the creed and for the first time turned it into a "rule of faith". The form in which the authority of Nicaea was expressed is significant. The Fathers believed they had the authority to express their faith through the words of a baptismal creed. We may partly believe Eusebius when he tells us that the baptismal creed of any particular church was the basis for their confession of faith, whatever the creed they may in fact have used.

This gives us a new type of creed or *symbolum*; they are rather tests of orthodoxy than baptismal confessions of faith, although of course these two functions are closely linked. The new element means that these creeds require theological labour to have gone before them, a self-reflexive language, an inquiry into the fundamentals of the faith and an episcopal confrontation. Among creeds of this kind the misleadingly named Nicaeno-Constantinopolitan Creed (proclaimed by the First Council of Constantinople) is the most highly developed. We may note that even though this creed contains non-biblical language it is an expression of the primitive faith. It expresses the single faith confessed by all the creeds of the individual churches.

The structure of these two formulae reveals their different origins. The Apostles' Creed confesses the eternal generation of the Word with the simple expression "and in Jesus Christ his only Son" and goes straight on to his incarnation, "born of the Holy Spirit". The Nicaeno-Constantinopolitan Creed, with polemical purposes in mind, stresses the nature of the Son and his mysterious origin in the bosom of the Father, "Light of light, begotten not made, being of one substance with the Father". The two creeds also differ in other significant details. The

Nicaeno-Constantinopolitan Creed has "resurrection of the flesh" instead of "resurrection from the dead" and "eternal life" instead of "life of the world to come". These changes show the passing from a Semitic to a more Hellenized mentality.

Furthermore, the Nicaeno-Constantinopolitan Creed has a whole series of phrases in apposition to "in the Holy Spirit" which are not found in any other creed to this day, with the exception of "he spake by the prophets" which is present in the Jerusalem Creed referred to by St Cyril about the year 350. These affirmations about the Holy Spirit are original elements peculiar to the Nicaeno-Constantinopolitan Creed, whereas the doctrine of the Spirit in the Apostles' Creed is barely developed at all.[2] Thus we see that the Apostles' Creed is properly speaking liturgical whereas the Nicaeno-Constantinopolitan Creed is technically theological. The older formula is more serene; the faith is being affirmed. The later is clearly polemical; orthodoxy is being defined. This brief comparison shows how the expression of the faith developed. We could say that this expression of faith begins with the phenomenology and proceeds to the logic of the faith, or, in more technical language, that it passes from statements in apposition to statements in logical connection, and from a movement of faith to an intellectual construction.

This gives rise to theological problems in the textual criticism of the creeds. Even in its earliest stage, Christian faith bears a dogmatic superstructure which seeks to define it in precise formulae as a safeguard against possible deformations. We may discern various stages between prayer and theology safeguarding the content of faith and the creed is one of these stages, which is why it can be seen as an authoritative formula, a "rule of faith". Moreover, these creeds began and were developed in very different circumstances. This has been shown well by Cullmann, although we do not have to accept the simplification that the primitive creed with its christological (or "economic") form corresponds to the preaching to the Jews, while the more elaborate creed with its trinitarian (or "theological") form corresponds to the preaching to the pagans.

[2] Cf. P. Nautin, *Je crois à l'Esprit Saint dans la sainte Eglise pour la résurrection de la chair* (Paris, 1947).

II. THE LITURGICAL CONTEXT AND THE THEOLOGICAL SIGNIFICANCE OF THE CREED

The Nicaeno-Constantinopolitan Creed was gradually introduced into the Eastern and Western liturgies, thus being restored to a context of worship. It slowly took the place of the individual creeds of individual churches and became universal. Through its liturgical use it regained its invocational and doxological character appropriate to the life of faith.[3] It would be a modern prejudice to say that because of its function as a declaration of faith, it was unsuited to worship and praise. Its objective language gains authenticity through its existential use as an act of faith by the believer. This is clearly what Bouillard means by the *"élan théologal"* of the creed[4] and it is most apparent in the worshipping context of the believing community. This impulse or movement of faith comes from the third article of the creed. Within the community, united in the Spirit, we believe in Christ and through him we encounter the first article of the creed, the almighty fatherhood of God. However, the movement is circular and can start from any of the articles of the creed, just as Paul begins his doxology with the grace of Christ, which reveals the love of the Father and is manifest in the fellowship of the Spirit.

It is this impulse or movement which explains what is meant by saying that the act of faith includes the journey towards the act of faith, so that "meaning is not separate from the approach which leads up to it; the approach is part of the meaning itself", as Levinas puts it.[5] Thus the creed is not primarily the acceptance of a set of propositions (that God exists, that Jesus is his Son, etc.), but it is an integral part of the dynamic movement of the mind towards God, who is completely different. Bouillard has no hesitation in saying that "the grammatical semantics of the creed serve to subordinate the doctrinal to the theological dynamism",[6]

---

[3] With reference to Nicaea, Thomas Camelot has shown that in the fourth century they spoke of the *faith* of Nicaea, never of the *creed* of Nicaea. Is it possible to see in this linguistic usage an indication that a dogmatic formula was converted into a baptismal creed? See "Symbole de Nicée ou foi de Nicée?", *Orient. Christ. Period.*, 13 (1947), pp. 425–33.

[4] H. Bouillard, "Le nom de Dieu dans le Credo", *L'analyse du langage théologique. Le nom de Dieu* (Paris, 1969), pp. 327–40.

[5] "La signification et le sens", *Revue de Métaphysique et de Morale*, 69 (1964), p. 135.   [6] *Op. cit.*, p. 328.

which is the movement of the spirit, or the being itself, towards God, who is infinitely different from everything we know from our experience. Historically the God of the language of the creed is not simply an object of knowledge; he reveals himself as a divine presence in the community. It was theologically necessary to speak objectively about this presence, although enormously dangerous because of the risk of loss and impoverishment which could be the result of a predominantly conceptual confession. The development of the faith is not merely a logical development. It is also a gradual opening to the mystery which we encounter in our life. However, statements about this opening process must be submitted to the rules of logic. Through the experience of contingency we encounter God the creator, just as reflection upon the history of Jesus the mediator illuminates for us the meaning of our own life directed towards the Father.

Furthermore, the theological or religious impulse which unites believers takes place in the human community to which the Spirit gives life. It is an impulse or movement bound by our own experience, mediated through our encounter with the history of Christ, and lived in the Spirit present in the Church. We confess them in the creed and through them come to God. The precise theological language used in a context of worship becomes invocation and praise. The purpose of the creed is not just to enlighten our minds but to lead us on the way to the Father. "Intellectual" faith is unauthentic if it is not based on the experience of contingency, from which we are freed by our encounter with Christ the Mediator. If he is not aware of his human frailty the Christian saying the creed, even if he understands it intellectually, will not reach God; he is merely repeating a lesson. The language of the creed is not didactic (the didactic form belongs to catechesis explaining the kerygma and preceding the proclamation of the faith). It is the language of confession which includes the experience of belief, an experience both personal and communal and concerned with a growing relationship between God and man.

III. From the Creed to the Anaphora

It is significant that the terminology of the early Church does not always distinguish clearly between the Eucharist and the creed. Sometimes the celebration of the Eucharist is described as a confession of faith (*contestatio* in Latin), while the confession is given the name Eucharist.

However, the language used in the Eucharist—and in particular in the text of the *anaphora*—and in the creed is different because it is language used for two different sacraments. Baptismal language is primarily the language of witness, while eucharistic language is for celebration and enriched with many sorts of signs, symbolical, ritual, conceptual and poetic. Although the object of faith is the same, the language of the creed and the *anaphora* has different resonances.

The Christian Eucharist, modelled on the Jewish blessing and the example of Jesus,[7] took a characteristic literary form, the language of "cultic discourse". In the early texts of the Eucharist the subject of this particular form of discourse is the same as that described in the religious tradition of Israel as the "wonders of Yahweh". In the Christian Eucharist, events related in the gospels have first place among these wonders, primarily, of course, the death and resurrection of Jesus. The new wonders worked by God in Jesus Christ are presented to the believing Christian as the crown of his ancient wonders which he wrought in the creation and in history. So the Christian Eucharist is a joyful celebration proclaiming that the limitations, ambiguities and deficiencies of human life and death itself have been conquered by the event of Christ. The memorial of this event, repeated ritually,[8] has a dimension of hope in the future culmination. These themes can be clearly discerned in early eucharistic prayers, although we do not have texts before the third century and historical analysis must be based on fragmentary allusions. The prayers in the *Didache* IX–X are not unanimously regarded as eucharistic; Justin's first *Apology* does not give us texts but merely a schema. The first text, the *anaphora* of Hippolytus'

[7] Cf. L. Ligier, "De la cène de Jésus à l'anaphore de l'Eglise", *La Maison-Dieu*, 87 (1966), pp. 7–51.

[8] Heidegger's concept of *repetition* can help us here. According to him, repetition leads to the actualization of the possibilities of the reality being repeated and thus to the achievement of its authentic content. The power of the repeated *memorial* leads to the discovery of its hidden inexhaustible meaning, and so becomes a questioning and critical hermeneutic of the rite.

Traditio apostolica, originated at the beginning of the third century. We do not find an abundance of texts until the fourth century and later and these are often very dissimilar from one another.[9]

According to the schema in Justin's first *Apology,* the eucharistic prayer praises "the Father in the name of the Son and of the Holy Spirit". This triple reference seems to make clear that it is the Christian Eucharist which is being described, although there are many documentary problems (sections are longer or shorter, there are repeats, changes of rhythm, changes in form of the blessing) and grammatical interruptions which bedevil interpretation. But the basic shape of the *anaphora* can be clearly seen in the oldest texts extant. We have the Syriac text of Addai and Mari and the Roman text of Hippolytus, both plainly of long standing and giving common witness, the more remarkable for their separate origins. They give a good idea of what the eucharistic prayer would have been like at its earliest stage. Hippolytus' text from *The Apostolic Tradition* does not correspond verbally at all, or hardly at all, with the *anaphora* of Addai and Mari, but it is easy to see the close likeness in the structure and themes of the two texts, as well as their common dependence on Jewish table prayers which have been Christianized. They both pass from thanksgiving for the creation to thanksgiving for the redemption, both have the same concept of the memorial although the words are not the same. The Semitic Christianity of Addai and Mari's *anaphora* could continue using the same terminology. But an *anaphora* for Greek-speaking Christians had to make clear that the memorial of Christ in the Eucharist was not merely subjective or psychological but a "making present" of the work of Christ. This inevitably meant the introduction of sacrificial language, which translated a Jewish "memorial" into a Hellenic "anamnesis".

Very generally, the new element in these eucharistic prayers, compared with Jewish table prayers, is faithfulness to the prayer of Jesus and his revelation. The Eucharist becomes more clearly defined. Later, as in the *anaphora* of Addai and Mari, liturgical themes are strengthened by more theological themes: celebration

[9] A. Hängai–I. Pahl, *Prex eucharistica. Textus e variis liturgiis antiquioribus selecti* (Fribourg, 1968).

(creation), thanksgiving (the divine economy), petition (*epiclesis* and doxology). These new elements are not rigidly structured but develop as the rhythm of a prayer which is both mono-theistic and trinitarian. It is the rhythmic movement of the *ana-phora* as a whole, analogous to the rhythm we noted in the baptismal creed. The dynamism of the economy of salvation, the joint work of the three divine persons, offers an existential rather than theological insight into the action of the Trinity. It is not an intellectual construction but a revealed mystery, which the Eucharist itself continues to reveal.

The liturgical expression of faith in the *anaphora* is enriched by the human experience it presupposes. God is praised as the creator. Creation, as the "presupposition of the covenant", finds its culmination in the mystery of Christ. The *anaphora*, taking as its starting-point the experience of man, God's collaborator in creation, recalls the mystery of love, in which the Christian shares in a community united by the Spirit (*epiclesis*). Every celebra-tion is a language spoken by men at a particular point in the biography of their faith, men living in the community of the Church. When this community gathers to celebrate the Euch-arist, this is the sign by which the Church in obedience to Christ seeks to show itself *as* the Church. One last aspect of the vitality of the faith is expressed in the *anaphora*. It would be false to assume that the ancient Eucharist was only praise of the creator and a memorial of the redeemer. Towards the end, as in the third and last *berakah* of the Jewish supper, this primitive Euch-arist, while recalling God's wonders, passes from praise to petition. And as in the third Jewish *berakah*, this prayer of petition which has come out of praise passes on into the final doxology.

IV. THE UNITY OF FAITH AND PLURALITY OF LITURGICAL FORMS

As we have seen from the above, there were many forms of the creed and from the third century onwards we have a variety of texts of the *anaphora*. An analysis of these formulations, which I have not been able to make here, suggests two important con-clusions. The first conclusion is that although we do not have many documents on the liturgy of the primitive community, this liturgy has a unique historical value because of its contact with apostolic times. We see that the deep *meaning* of the confession of faith or eucharistic act of thanksgiving, although expressed in various ways from one church to another, is remarkably fixed. The primitive community was not bound by a single form, but it was bound by a single idea, which meant that although there were many variations in detail, the spirit and general conduct of the celebration were basically extremely similar.

Throughout the Church from Syria to Rome we find fixed fundamentals which are always attributed to the apostles. But side by side with these we also find forms of expression suited to different mentalities. Nowadays we would say that there was a single liturgical content with a number of free rubrics. However, as the celebration is still very simple and accidental elements have hardly crept in at all, the variety of expression is not in fact very great. Thus we have basic unity together with freedom of expression.[10] This dualism does present a serious difficulty because of one of the laws governing the historical development of the phenomenon of religion. According to this law, every small modification in the cult eventually reflects on the perception of the faith by the faithful, and introduces into the faith a modification corresponding to the modification of the service of worship. And the reverse is also true; every modification in the faith is reflected sooner or later in the liturgy. Of course no faith is ever transmitted in a pure state. In fact history and anthropology only have examples on one situation: that of a faith passed on in a religious tradition which also contains its own liturgical model. Perhaps the answer to our own problem can be found in the simplicity and concentrated (= directed towards the centre, Christ) nature of both the faith and liturgy of the primitive community.

The second conclusion that we may draw from our analysis of the early texts is this. In the liturgy, the Church not only expresses its faith. The wealth and variety of its symbols and songs show that it also lived the faith in festive celebration. The liturgy is not just a theoretical announcement but an action. This action expresses a conviction and at the same time develops this conviction and communicates it to others. The symbolic action com-

---

[10] For the Eucharist, see L. Ligier, "La struttura della preghiera eucaristica: diversità e unità", *Eph. liturgicae*, 82 (1968), pp. 191–215.

municates the whole of a reality, not only that part of it which can be grasped by the intelligence. It recognizes and passes on a heritage, which contains more than the individual consciousness of the worshippers. The personal experience of faith, which may be weak or strong, is embodied in an action of the community and enacted in a social context. In this way the liturgy introduces us to Christian truth by a personal communion, through action and through prayer, by means of a familiar ritual practised by men living in faith and love. It does not introduce us to this truth by means of discourse and argument, but by a living celebration through which we perceive the presence of him whom we wish to know and recognize. The richly varied language of the liturgy includes all the ways in which men communicate with one another. These suggestions might help to re-establish the historical sense of the well-known phrase *legem credendi statuit lex orandi*. The *lex orandi* is not simply the liturgy—it is also the gospel precept to pray without ceasing. This means believing in the need for the free grace of God, that is the *lex credendi*. A *lex credendi* which includes the uncertainty and the risk of faith, goes beyond dogmatic security and has its place at the deepest level of experience of God's presence and his absence. We see many things because we have prayed and struggled with them. This is true of the God invoked in the creed and Christ represented in the Eucharist. So we should not be surprised that the primitive baptismal and eucharistic texts, on this interpretation, are a starting-point for studying many current problems of the experience and expression of the faith in both liturgy and theology.

Translated by Dinah Livingstone

Language of Worship

(a) *The Poetics of Faith in the Liturgy*

Jean-Pierre Manigne

WE SHALL deal with liturgy in this article in so far as it makes use of a poetics of faith. In other words, we shall widen the question of worship to include the expressiveness of faith of which liturgy is simply one manifestation, but at the same time we shall indicate certain barriers between liturgy and certain similar modes of expression which give colour and substance to any celebration, but which can never be confused with a believing celebration. We can only do the preparatory work for this process here, but it should probably be carried out by means of several convergent investigations. In our view, some of the present difficulties and dead-ends are the result of forgetting both the openness of the liturgy (towards what overshadows it or goes beyond it) and its limitations within the linguistic area. We must therefore try to establish the "position" of the liturgy from theological and cultural references which will determine its location and indicate its boundaries.

I. LITURGICAL CRITERIA

Liturgy is meaningful. Any act of worship can be defined as a totality of the *signs* by means of which a certain number of *things signified* as the result of a common belief are communicated, by means of a certain number of *signifiers*, to a definite religious community. It will easily be seen that this definition does away with too vague a view of celebration and enables us to look for criteria. It is true that, in one respect, our history weighs heavily upon us. We are part of a history which has been dominated by the almost universal tendency to experience the fashions, gestures and laws of celebration according to the norms laid down by a caste of initiates which monopolized the knowledge of the group. There is an unholy link between ritual and clerical imperialism. If the word (as proclamation, communication or dialogue) is of its nature progressive, ritual is of its nature conservative.

Since Christian worship is both word and ritual, we should not be surprised to find that it gives rise to great tension between conservatism and progress. Today in practice it is one of the main points of confrontation, one of the last forums in which Christians of differing political convictions and no other point of contact can meet.

Ritual also gives rise to great ambiguity in the case of the individual, since man can never celebrate the object of his belief without exposing himself; in ritual he removes his mask, and yet this revelation can always be rejected in the very name of the transcendence which the ritual claims to celebrate. Ritual is that paradoxical act in which the *revelatum* always has the power to blind.

If we consider only the Christian liturgy, in connection with the questions about it raised today, we find that the contradictions, both for the community of believers and for each individual member of that community, and the fundamental ambiguity which leads to the prejudices and ideologies betrayed in practice by the "style" of the celebration being attributed to the absolute professed by faith, are today being naturally aggravated by the weakening of the canonical norms which until recently had enabled us to avoid the crisis by imposing a double series of criteria. There were firstly the criteria of orthodoxy which established the criteria for membership of the group, such as excommunication (in all its shades of meaning), and secondly the criteria of orthopraxis which established norms according to which the celebration should take place.

The artificial or arbitrary character of these two sets of criteria is today suspect, but it would be a mistake to tar with the same brush fact and law. It is true that the criteria (both of orthodoxy and orthopraxis) can no longer be decreed in such an abstract way, but nor can any believing community do without a minimum of declared norms without abandoning its own identity.

Since the criteria of orthodoxy, which determine membership, do not, at least directly, concern us, we shall try to elucidate the conditions necessary for orthopraxis. Given agreement on membership, it remains to give that membership proper manifestation. In other words, we could put the question in this way: "What liturgy is appropriate to the community of believers?"

Our first step will be an attempt to understand what is signified in such a question, that is, the community of believers in so far as it is called to reveal itself to its members (the pastoral aspect) and becomes a visible question for those outside it (the missionary aspect). In a second stage we shall consider the liturgy as a *ritual activation, the signifier of this object signified*.

II. The Church as the Dwelling-Place of Believers and a Sign for the Nations

To define the Church as a "dwelling-place" and a "sign" is to talk of it as something visible, and also to distinguish this visible aspect from the false appearances into which the Church constantly falls through unbelief or natural lethargy. A dwelling-place and a sign are not to be confused with a state, a society, a hierarchy or a legal system.

The dwelling-place is the place where those who feel at home can live together, and the sign is a possible answer when men who are not yet at home in the dwelling-place ask about the ultimate meaning of their destiny. This question may be formally universal, but it is not so in fact. Similarly, if the sign offered by the Church remains open to universality in a formal sense, it cannot and should not aim at factual universality here and now. The difference between the formal and the factual indicates that what is involved is an historical reality. The Church has no kind of all-embracing view of this history; it is involved in it and entirely responsible only to men who are trying to live by faith and to those who are looking for a faith to live by. The Church does not provide an actual answer for the latter. This explanation is called for by our question. What we have said is that, by trying to show itself in the universality it claims, the

Church loses the possibility of providing a dwelling-place here and now for those who are trying to live by faith and ceases to be a sign recognizable by those who are looking for a faith to live by.

This dwelling-place and this sign are formed by the poetics of faith, that is, according to the poetic movement proper to the irreducibly historical manifestation of the kingdom. We shall try to understand this manifestation in four different ways: by considering the mystery of the incarnation, the meaning of parable and sacrament, and finally the environment offered by the community of believers.

1. *The Incarnation—Foundation of the Church as a Dwelling-Place and a Sign*

If the incarnation is indeed the mystery in which the Word—"he who was from the beginning"—"came to dwell amongst us", we may suggest, as one of the chief "marks" of this mystery, its character of mediation between the highest transcendence and the closest familiarity. This mediation does not operate by half-measures, standing at an equal distance from both extremes, but is the source of a co-existence of the extremes. This co-existence is visible and tangible. We remember the opening of 1 John—the basis of our message, our evidence, is not an intuition, an illumination, a common spirit, an idea of God or a worldly ideology, but rather a life which was touched, heard and seen, eternal life become a face, the mortal and risen body of Jesus of Nazareth.

This is to say, the possibility of the Church's existence and mission begins with a person and, as a result of this, the style both of the Church's assemblies and of the mission to the world cannot be immaterial. The incarnation does not simply determine the content or the meaning of this assembly and this mission—it also determines their mode.

There is therefore room in the theological disciplines for aesthetic reflection, a reflection whose purpose is to clarify the status conferred on the appearances, gestures and words of the community of believers, by the "face" of the incarnation. What dwelling-place does it allow them to occupy, what sign does it give them to display? We shall take the language of parable and the sacramental system as two aspects of this expression of faith through which the meaning and style of the incarnation continue to be manifested, and we shall speak of the community as where this manifestation takes place.

2. Parabolic Expression

In parables a certain reality is manifested in a certain way. The reality is that of the kingdom, which means that of a God who is totally other ("my thoughts are not your thoughts nor my ways your ways"), drawing near. The mode is that of the familiar story (indicating the proximity), but with a paradox (indicating the otherness). There is a vineyard owner, but one who pays the last workers as much as the first comers and sends his son to the place where his workmen have been killed. There is a shepherd, but one who leaves his flock in the wilderness for the sake of a single sheep. A rich man gives a banquet but invites all the filthy wretches from the street-corners.

The climate of parable introduces the inhabitants of the dwelling-place to the dimension of gratuitousness and makes them live in the awareness of the absolute liberality summed up in the saying, "All that is mine is yours". For the others, the parable sets up the "sign" of this gratuitousness; it offers them the chance to enter in their turn into a community in which this strange economy with its initiatives and transgressions of the normal rules of exchange is now the norm.

3. Sacramental Expression

In sacraments a certain reality is manifested in a certain mode. The reality is that of the covenant, that is, a reconciliation the initiative for which comes from above. The mode is the taking of the elements (bread, wine, water, oil), gestures and actions of ordinary life (the meeting of a man and woman, a meal, confession and forgiveness). As the *urbs sacramentum*, the Church keeps the inhabitants of the dwelling-place within the sphere of this reconciliation and keeps them aware of it. By doing this it opens to them the possibility of a renewed use of the world, of food, sexuality, growth, illness and death, and for the others it raises the sign of this reconciliation.

4. *The Community Environment*

The community we are talking about is not autonomous. Its reality does not lie in itself, but in the one who brings it together; it is the community of those attracted by the economy of the parables, a sacramental community. Nevertheless it has its own mode of assembly and operation. The mode or style of the sacrament and that of the parable develop and become established by entering the community life which is its natural environment and the purpose of which is constantly to bring the message and the promise to their most specific realization.

The mode of this manifestation of the community is therefore specific, and cannot be confused with that of other associations devoted to any other aim than the realization just mentioned. The believing community builds the walls of its own dwelling-place with living stones, and to the degree that the work progresses it is missionary, that is, it is meaningful to the stranger in search of a house.

It would be a misunderstanding if we were taken as contrasting the sign and the dwelling-place, because the people of the dwelling live in it as a sign and the sign never points to anything other than a dwelling.

III. THE LITURGY AS A SYMBOLIC ACTIVITY

The incarnation, the proclamation of life in the parabolic mode, the sacramental system, community: all these are examples of the manifestation of faith, and each would require a discussion of its components, but we have mentioned them here because they seem to us to be the basis of believing poetics, a poetics of faith considered from the point of view of what it derives from its own origin, the faces, words, gestures and places of its manifestation. Liturgy comes in here. It is made up of faces, words and actions; it opens up a place and brings it to life. It can be defined as the symbolic actualization of the reality of the Church to the extent that this is embodied in faith and becomes visible to men.

To say that the liturgy is essentially symbolic indicates both its privilege and its limitations. It has the privilege of a symbol in being an initiation; for those who approach it, it opens up a possibility of which it offers here and now the realization in symbol, in this case, the reconciliation of men with God and with each other. It has the limitations of the symbol in that the fulfilment it presents is not actually complete in itself. This is not because the symbol is not itself realistic and effective, but because its effectiveness requires the whole of life, including its most prosaic fringes, to develop its effectiveness. The liturgy symbolically effects what remains for us to do. Failure to understand this can change the essential truth of the celebration.

To say that the liturgy is an actualization implies that what is to be signified in it cannot be revealed without an effort of intelligence and imagination on our part. We will take three examples of this actualization, language, spectacle and festival. These three approaches will also be three ways of showing where we think the distinctive character of the liturgy of faith lies as compared with language, spectacle and festival in the "world".

1. *Liturgical Language*

Three languages, or, better, three functions of language, are involved here—communication, expression and communion.

Any attempt to establish a strict distinction between expression and communication would be a piece of futile formalism. What we want to do here is not to separate different areas but to indicate the poles which give language its real direction, according to whether the main purpose is to spread a piece of information (and also to spread it accurately) or to express a certain relation to the world, one which affects us at a depth we find it hard to reach so that the communication of this half-perceived reality is a secondary concern. The first function dominates everyday language, and the press, radio and television. In the second case we are dealing with the less common language of confidences, bordering on soliloquy, and that of modern poetry.

Too often today the language of worship oscillates between these two "modes", neither of which can express it fully. We must try to see the nostalgia embodied by each of these languages in its own way, and see how it leads us towards a third type of language with a function and style of its own which could be called the language of communion.

To commune is more than to communicate, but it is also more than self-expression. To be in communion with each other means to ensure not only that pieces of information but also that experiences and attitudes coincide. It means not losing anything of that substance which poetic language deals with privately (a threefold relation to the world, to others and to fate illustrated by creative expression), and at the same time associating that threefold relation, the covenant created by the imagination with the covenant experienced simultaneously by our brothers in the faith.

What has already been said about the contradictions and ambiguities we experience at present in liturgical celebrations will have made it clear that this is difficult to put into practice, but it would be a considerable advance if it were recognized that it is a distinctive aim, and that between the languages of communication, of expression tied to subjectivity and the language of communion there is a genuine solution in continuity. At present this continuity is not recognized; people refuse to see that these three languages are not extensions of each other. In fact, in order to speak any of them and give priority to any one of the three functions, we must start each time from a different point, a different source. For language dedicated primarily to communication, the source is the linguistic community in which information circulates, and for information about this community we turn to sociology. Language dedicated primarily to expression comes from the solitude of the creator in which other solitudes will also be reflected; to describe this source is the task of literary criticism. The source of the language of communion is the community, and if it is a believing community the description of the community is theology. This shows us the indissoluble connection between the question of orthodoxy, which tries to recognize the place of communion, and the question of orthopraxis, which asks what language is appropriate to the place once it has been recognized.

Of course, distinguishing these three functions is not meant in an exclusive sense; communion, after all, has to be expressive and communicative. Our aim is to allow the world of faith to exist as a specific universe, not a separate one.

2. The Liturgy as Spectacle

It may be surprising to treat the liturgy as a spectacle when the rediscovery of the role of the whole community in the celebration excludes the category of spectator, but by calling the liturgy a spectacle all we mean is that it offers something to see. After trying to say where the source of the liturgical word was to be found, we must now try to describe the distinctive character of its visual aspect.

If we remember what is symbolically actualized in the liturgy, we realize that the spectacle we are concerned with here has to reveal the nearness of an event normally quite beyond the reach of our everyday sight. The familiarity of the liturgical spectacle, which uses the simplest things—a meal, washing, gestures of reconciliation—is totally subordinate to a message which shatters that familiarity. These two characteristics of the liturgy which are generally opposed, solemnity and ordinariness, are in fact necessary components of the liturgical manifestation. A proper celebration is one which allows the solemnity of the event to be seen through the very familiarity of the attitudes and objects. It is certainly easier to destroy than to represent this tension between the solemn and the ordinary, but it is only by respecting it that the liturgical signs can avoid betraying what they signify.

The best analogy for such a manifestation is the face, a "spectacle" which cannot tolerate an indifferent spectator, since it is not so much observed as an observer. In the same way a real liturgy immediately destroys the spectacles with which it is classified. It detaches itself from undifferentiated space by directing our attention towards the event which it commemorates. It spiritually overflows the very matter which supports and expresses it, and cannot be contained in it. Finally, at the very moment when we observe we are observed, our look turns back to meet and question us. We must constantly ask ourselves if the celebration we initiate in fact achieves this threefold manifestation. Does it really take hold of our attention? Can it free itself from its own image by taking us into an area of spiritual liberty totally out of proportion to the confined space in which the rite unfolds? Finally, does it succeed in transforming the spectacle into a meeting?

3. *The Liturgy as a Festival*

Finally, the liturgy is a festival, in other words, it gives us not only something to hear and see but also something to live. A festival always celebrates the effervescence man carries within him, or collectively, that which a society carries within it. We can speak of the power and ambiguity of festivity. The power of a festival can bring to an even greater heat not only what we think we are, but all that we are; it brings into the interplay of relations and exchanges the most secret part of our hearts, of which we ourselves are unaware. The ambiguity is coextensive with the power. If what is brought to boiling-point in the festivity is already there beforehand, we must expect festivity to bring into the open the worse as well as the better. It is not enough for personal or collective alienation to be revealed in order to be cured; it must come to the surface in a place which can liberate it. The Christian festival therefore cannot really take place without opening in repentance and ending in conversion. These are two conditions as far removed as possible from moralism, which refuses to allow the hidden depths of the heart and will to come into the open and go free, and also from the secular celebrations which communities of believers too often take as the model for their festivals.

A festival of faith will make room for the sins of the faithful. It will address itself to the whole of man and therefore prefer forms of celebration which reveal him in his entirety; but it cannot accept sin without making known its remission, and the price of that remission.

IV. Conclusion

We have done no more than begin an investigation which must be continued in two different directions, that of the faith which is the source of what is signified in the liturgy and that of the community which celebrates that faith by recognizing it in the signifiers which transmit it for the benefit of the community. The assimilation between the object signified and these signifiers is part of the pledge involved in any communion; it is its visible features. Without confusing this with a completely transparent theological communion, between each believer and

God and between the believers themselves, we may feel that such an assimilation is very unlikely to be achieved without any exceptional achievement of the theological communion, and that ordinary conditions allow only an approximation to this. On the other hand, an authentic communion may certainly coexist with a seriously inadequate liturgical manifestation—this has been seen in the past and can still be seen—but this situation is in itself a scandal. A deeper exploration of what is signified in our liturgies and the adjustment of the signifiers to that object signified are therefore together a fundamental pastoral and missionary task.

Translated by Francis McDonagh

(b) *The Performativity of Liturgical Language*

Jean Ladrière

INTRODUCTION: THE PROBLEM SITUATED

THE expression of faith in worship relies upon various registers which may be reduced to three: those of vocal, gestural and symbolic expression. *Vocal expression* is one form of language use, which may involve singing. *Gestural expression* is a form of body language—the body as a meaningful force. *Symbolic expression* is a way of using things (places, clothes, lights, and so on) which endows them with a referential capacity over and above their direct meaning. These three forms of expression are mutually supportive, and any full analysis of expressive worship obviously ought to take into account the complex ways in which they interact. I shall restrict my remarks here to language in the strict sense of the word. More exactly, I shall concern myself with the ways in which linguistic analysis can help us to understand the expression of faith in liturgy.

I. Some Constituents of Language Analysis

The basic problem is to discover how liturgical language works. Clearly this kind of language cannot be analysed in terms proper to information theory: it does not consist in the reporting of events, the description of objects, the formulation of theoretical hypotheses, the statement of experimental findings, or the handing on of data. It is characterized in that it is a certain form of action; it puts something into practice: in short, it possesses an "operativity". It is not merely a verbal commentary on an action external to itself; in and of itself, it is action.

1. *Constative Statements and Performative Statements*

In order to describe it appropriately, one might, then, use Austin's well-known distinction between constative and performative statements.[1] A *constative statement* merely reports a certain state of affairs, communicates a certain datum of knowledge, affirms that these or those objects are behaving in this or that way, that this or that event took place in one way or another, that this was the result of that particular experiment, and so on. A *performative statement*, by virtue solely of its enunciation, performs a certain kind of action. For example, if X says to Y: "I promise to help you in your enterprise", X engages himself effectively to take those steps in the future which are necessary to help Y in his enterprise. Hence X creates a new situation which did not exist before the moment in which he stated his promise, and which exists in no way other than by virtue of that promise: he is now bound by the obligation which he assigned to himself. Similarly, if X says to Y: "Thank you for your help", he makes explicit for Y an attitude of acknowledgment that he has towards him; he so to speak makes effective this attitude in putting himself, in regard to Y, in the position of the person obliged. The very enunciation of this sentence brings into existence a relationship of a certain type between X and Y. In enunciating the sentence in question, X does not describe an inward state; he does not simply acquaint Y with a feeling that he experiences in re-

---

[1] J. L. Austin, *Philosophical Papers*, ed. Urmson and Warnock (Oxford, 1961) and *How to do Things with Words*, ed. Urmson (Oxford, 1962).

gard to him, but commits himself in a characteristic manner in regard to Y. The enunciation of the sentence is a veritable action. In order, therefore, to express the operative (non-descriptive) nature of liturgical language, we may use the term "performativity", as proposed by Austin. The problem with which we are faced is one of determining the exact kind of performativity proper to liturgical language.

2. *Syntax, Semantics, Pragmatics*

This question has to be stated in terms of what may be taken as given in the field of linguistic analysis. It has become customary in the study of language, as Charles Morris suggested,[2] to distinguish between three areas: syntax, semantics and pragmatics. *Syntax* is concerned with the ways in which language is structured, that is: the ways in which the constituent units combine to form complex wholes, and the relations existing between elements: for example, the relation between subject and predicate, or between a noun and its qualifier. *Semantics* studies the forms and mechanisms of meaning. *Pragmatics* is concerned with the relations between language units and their users. The problem of the performativity of language is one, initially, of pragmatics, since it considers the users. On the other hand, it is also a matter of semantics, inasmuch as it concerns the meaning of performative verbs. Hence the characteristic mode of action of the verb "to promise" determines the meaning of this verb. The distinction between semantics and pragmatics is not, therefore, absolutely clear-cut, and recent developments in pragmatics indeed suggest a fusion of the two viewpoints in a more general context. Nevertheless, it is certain that the performative aspects of language essentially involve speakers and those spoken to.

3. *The Theory of "Speech Acts"*

The concept of performativity also has to be more exactly elucidated. Austin himself found it necessary to extend the distinction between constative and performative: he remarked that *every* statement has a performative aspect. (In a statement which

[2] C. W. Morris, *Foundations of the Theory of Signs* (Chicago, 1938).

is merely the enunciation of a verification there is in fact an implied act of assertion. In making such a statement one carries out a specific action which consists in postulating this proposition as an affirmation that one holds to be true.) This led Austin to introduce the concept of an "illocutory force": any statement, quite apart from its own meaningful content, effects a certain type of operation; it so to speak displays a specific linguistic effectiveness. On the basis of this concept, John R. Searle developed a theology of "speech acts" which throws much light on the operative nature of language.[3] Searle's goal is the elucidation not of language as an object in itself, independent of its users, but of the use of language. His basic viewpoint is as follows: to speak a language is to take part in a form of behaviour governed by rules: in other words, to perform certain acts in accordance with certain rules. Searle distinguishes four kinds of speech act: acts of *enunciation* (consisting in the enunciation of words and sentences), *propositional acts* (consisting in acts of predication, which result in the attribution of properties to objects which are spoken about, and in reference acts, which give indications that enable one more or less precisely to identify the objects one is speaking about), *illocutionary acts* (consisting in the accomplishment of a specific linguistic operation: for example, affirmation, description, interrogation, thanks, promising, ordering, asking, approving, recommending, deciding, and so on), and *perlocutionary acts* (consisting in the production of a certain effect in those addressed: for example, persuading, enlightenment, inspiration, and so on . . .). The decisive point is that a propositional act cannot occur in an isolated state: it is the necessary adjunct of an illocutionary act. (In addition, these acts become explicit thanks only to an act of enunciation, and the illocutionary act is associated with a prolocutionary act, in so far as it may have a specific effect on the hearer.) Illocutionary acts are clarified, at the enunciation level, by indicators with an illocutionary power. These are expressions which invoke the use of performative verbs, for example: "I affirm this . . .", and so on; "I wish that", and so forth. These indicators are often taken

[3] John R. Searle, *Speech Acts: An Essay in the Philosophy of Language* (Cambridge, 1970).

as understood, but it is always possible to elicit them. Hence a constative sentence such as "It is rainy" should be stated in a complete form as "I affirm that the weather is rainy." The general form of an illocutionary act would, therefore, be F (p), where the symbol F can be replaced by a symbol of illocutionary power, and the symbol p by a proposition (in the ordinary sense of the word). The proposition involves predicates (which occur in the acts of predication) and referential terms (put into effect in the acts of reference). Therefore it expresses a certain state of things. The illocutionary indicator shows what kind of operation relates to the content expressed by the proposition. For instance, take the sentence: "Will you lend me your pen?" This sentence may be explicated as follows: "I ask you to lend me your pen." Here there is, on the one hand, the illocutionary indicator "I ask", which shows what kind of performativity is characteristic of the sentence, and, on the other hand, the proposition "X lends his pen to Y", where X and Y are referential terms which refer respectively to the addressee and to the speaker, and where "lend his pen" is a relational predicate (expressing a specific relation between X and Y).

II. The Illocutionary Force of Liturgical Language

This theory of speech acts enables us to reformulate our problem more precisely, as follows: What is the characteristic illocutionary power of sentences in liturgical language? It is immediately clear that this question does not admit of a simple answer (at least if one is to retain the notion of "illocutionary power" in the precise sense which it is employed in Searle's theory.

(a) *The specific complexity of liturgical language and its unifying principle*

Liturgical language is very complex. It can feature sentences which are tantamount to being exhortations, and others which are confessional in form ("I acknowledge..."); others which are interrogative, others which are adulatory, some which are cast in the form of statements of belief; others which are expressed as wishes; and yet others which take an imperative form.

A more exact analysis would extend this list, and introduce distinctions within the categories thus produced. In this way one could obtain a more or less adequate categorization of the illocutionary forms of liturgical language. But even this would only be a first step towards a proficient categorization. It is important to realize how the diverse illocutionary forms accord with one another; how, together, they make up one language, which definitively constitutes the totality of liturgical language. This unity would seem to be neither of the syntactical nor of the semantic order, but of a pragmatic type: it is the kind of operativity characteristic of liturgical language which ordains its specificity and unites its diverse constituents. Hence one might return to the question already posed, but this time allowing the term "performativity" a generalized meaning: What is the characteristic performativity of liturgical language? This question must refer, not to the sentences which go to make up liturgical language, taken individually, but to that language itself, to the general principle by which it functions. Hence the term "performativity" should no longer be understood in the sense of a "determined illocutionary form" but in the sense of a "general principle of operativity". Only on the basis of this principle is it possible to understand not only how the particular illocutionary acts which occur in liturgical language are united, but the characteristic suasions which affect them in the context of this language. (Hence petitions do not give effect to just any interrogative acts; it is a matter of prayers: what has to be specified is what exactly makes a petition a prayer.) Therefore every effort must be made to conceive liturgical language as a whole, or as the general context within which such sentences function—an initial analysis of which might reveal the specific illocutionary forces at work.

(b) *The threefold performativity of liturgical language*

My initial proposition of course calls for additional illustrations and more detailed explanation. If liturgical language is considered as a whole, it would seem to possess a threefold performativity: that of an existential induction, that of an institution, and that of a "presentification". These three modes of performativity are reciprocal; the most decisive, that which unites liturgical language, is "presentification".

1. *Existential Induction*

By "existential induction" is meant an operation by means of which an expressive form awakens in the person using it a certain affective disposition which opens up existence to a specific field of reality. Of course an effect is in question, and therefore the "perlocutionary" aspect of language; what has to be studied is the means by which this effect is produced: what exactly is the kind of language function which enables it to produce such an effect. This question, of course, has to do with its performativity. To be sure, in order to elucidate this question, one has both to examine the role of personal pronouns and the occurrence of certain performative verbs.

Personal pronouns have a wholly characteristic function in language. They so to speak indicate, in relation to what is said, the "places" which can be occupied by the language users. Therefore they are neither predicative nor referential terms (as nouns are). They are instead a kind of indeterminate indicator which enables linguistic operations to be connected with actors and hence make possible the affective functioning of language as behaviour—as the effecting of specific acts. The "I" of first-person personal pronouns indicates the "place", in conversation, of an individual speaker. In pronouncing the word "I", the speaker to some extent takes on himself those operations which are implicit in the proposition which he enunciates. He relates to himself the diverse speech acts by virtue of which this sentence can function as multi-meaningful. These acts are not arbitrary, but are controlled by exact rules revealed by linguistic analysis; the very presence of these rules gives language its objective character and makes it an instrument of expression and communication of universal reference. But, to be effective, these rules have to be used by someone. In using the first person, the speaker employs the constitutive rules of language; in one sense he submits to these rules, but in another sense he gives them life. The rules in themselves could never give rise to conversation—to discourse. It is by virtue of the speaker that they become operative, that those acts are produced in and by which they effectively exercise their constitutive function.

Second-person pronouns indicate the position of those addressed, hence the function of the "you" in the expression "I ask you" is to indicate that the question is oriented to the person addressed by the speaker. The same formula can obviously be used for any addressee. Only the context (both linguistic and non-linguistic) determines who is the person who represents the term "you". Through the mediation of this term, the conversation becomes an effective means of communication—a "location of interlocution". By means of first-person pronouns the conversation becomes discourse for someone; it is, so to speak, rooted in a concrete act, in which a speaker takes part (in accordance with the illocutionary form characteristic of that which he enunciates). For second-person pronouns, the conversation becomes speech addressed to someone—an element of a dialogic relationship.

Liturgical language makes especial use of "us" and "thou". The plural form, in "we" and "us", indicates that there is a number of speakers, but that they are acting collectively, as if there were only one speaker. Here we are concerned with the second kind of performativity of liturgical language: *institution*. This language, in the special way proper to the use of "we", institutes a community. The "thou" is not a physically present person. Liturgical language is addressed to God. This is clear, linguistically, from the context in which the "thou" occurs: e.g., by use of the term "Lord", but also by the repetition of liturgical language.

Liturgical language uses certain characteristic performative verbs, such as "to ask", "to pray", "to give thanks". Often these verbs are understood: imperative formulations involve a non-expressed performative. (Hence such a declaration as "Lord, hear us" may be explicated as "Lord, we beg you to hear us".) Such verbs express illocutionary acts presupposing certain attitudes: trust, veneration, gratitude, submission, contrition, and so on. These attitudes come into effect at the very moment when, by virtue of the enunciation of the sentence, the corresponding act takes place. The performative verb is not a description of the attitude which its enunciation presupposes; its function is not to indicate the existence of this attitude, but is, so to speak, the attitude itself: it makes it exist in an effective manner by virtue of the illocutionary act underlying its enunciation.

These observations show that liturgical language is an "existential inductor". Through the mediation of the "we", the members of the liturgical community assume certain illocutionary acts and the attitudes which they presuppose. On the other hand, in using the second-person pronoun, the "thou", they take as their addressee that very One who speaks to them in the texts of the liturgy, and who is designated by terms of invocation such as "Lord" and "Father". The attitudes help to give these words their meaning, and by their own connotations these terms specify the range of those attitudes. These attitudes form a system: they reinforce one another and in their very reciprocity constitute a basic disposition, which, precisely because it is a disposition, is of an affective, and not a representative, order. In its very functioning, liturgical language is the putting into effect of certain specific acts which have their repercussion in the affectivity of the speakers. The term "affectivity" is used here in a very basic sense. It is not a question of emotion, nor really of feeling, but of that form of constitutive receptivity which makes us capable of adjusting to reality in its several manifestations: to the reality of salvation which comes to us from God by the mediation of Jesus Christ, who is announced in the texts of Scripture and is accomplished in the words of the Canon, and received in the words of the action of grace. All these words prepare the soul to hear what they propose and effect. One might say that by virtue of them what at first was only a kind of readiness, vague and undifferentiated, expressed simply by presence in the place where the liturgy is celebrated, gradually takes on a more definite and concrete form, and becomes like a state of agreement between the soul and the mystery that takes place. It is in this very agreement that this mystery becomes present for those who are taking part in it. Hence it prefigures, and in a certain way already realizes that which this mystery in its present action already anticipates.

2. *Institution*

The effect of liturgical language as institution is not only to dispose souls to welcome that which it suggests, but, by the same means, to institute a community. In pronouncing the "we", each of the participants to some extent takes upon himself the acts which occur at the same moment, and by virtue of the same words, by all the others. These acts obey very exact rules. They have specific characters and do not depend on the arbitrary impulse of any one speaker. The participants meet in a kind of objective space determined by their speech acts. The community is initiated in this meeting. Here one may speak of an induction effect. Language is not the expression of a community constituted before it and apart from it and is not the description of what such a community would be, but the location in which and the instrument by means of which the community is constituted. In so far as it gives to all participants—as co-locutors—the chance to take on the same acts, it establishes between them that operative reciprocity which constitutes the reality of a community.

There are also the contents to which the illocutionary acts refer and to which certain definite propositional acts correspond. Liturgical language does not consist only of acts of request or acknowledgment. It asks for specific things (e.g., that "your kingdom come"); it thanks for precise benefits. Hence it makes present a certain reality. It is that reality, accomplished in and by the liturgy, which establishes the community. For the actual community which says the words of the liturgy, which receives from these very words its cohesion, unity quality of community, is only a constituent cell of that infinitely greater community to which the liturgical action refers, and which is also in part constructed from it. In assuming the acts of language in which the liturgy obtains its efficacy, the participants take on that mystery of unification which brings them together in the communion of saints. This mystery is the mystery of the body of Christ. By sharing in the liturgical meal, in which Christ gives his body as food, the participants are incorporated in him and thus become true members of his body. This ultimate reality of the community is no longer properly speaking of the order of language. But it is signified by language and it is therefore possible to see by what mechanisms it announces that of which it is the sign.

3. Presentification

The most fundamental aspect of the performativity of liturgical language is presentification. By all those acts which it effects, this language makes present for the participants, not as a spectacle, but as a reality whose efficacy they take into their very own life, that about which it speaks and which it effects in diverse ways: that is, the mystery of Christ, his life and his death, and his resurrection: the revelation conveyed to us in him of the mystery of God: the accomplishment of the eternal plan by virtue of which we are called to become children of God, co-heirs of Christ in eternal life. This mystery is not made present by liturgical language in the same way as descriptive language which pictures forth that of which it speaks. Instead it endows it so to speak with its own operativity (i.e., that of the acts which make it up), in order to become operative for the community established by the liturgy. This effect is produced in several ways.

(a) *Repetition*

In some of its parts liturgy repeats texts which announce, either as an event that is to come or as an event that has already oc-curred in Jesus Christ, the mystery of salvation. Repetition is not a mere quotation but the resumption into acts of today of words written or spoken at a given moment in the past. What is handed down is merely prescriptions for acts that are to be carried out. When a speaker takes up these indications, he puts into effect the acts they prescribe and the word spoken in the texts then be-comes once more living in his own words. There is something like a superimposition of two kinds of effectiveness: that proper to the speaker and that proper to the text itself, or more exactly to the words it schematizes. The speaker allows the revelatory essence of the original words to emerge. He makes the message of the words his food. In re-forming the words which announce the mystery of salvation, the liturgical community actively enters into the mystery which thus becomes effective in that com-munity.

(b) *Proclamation*

The culmination of this process might be said to come in the confession of faith. This takes the form of a proclamation, whose illocutionary power is that of an attestation, ratification and commitment. That which the creed declares is the mystery of salvation. In enunciating this mystery it makes it present and active, and so to speak makes it appear in the space of its own words. By means of propositional acts, the confession of faith brings into existence a form of discursive articulation in which the very content of the mystery becomes manifest.

(c) *Sacramentality*

But it is clearly in its sacramental aspect that liturgical language has its most profoundly actualizing effect. In repeating the words of the Last Supper, the celebrant does more than commemorate it. He repeats once again that which Christ did, in giving again to the words which Christ used that efficacy which Christ gave them, in conferring on them again the power to do what they mean. This is something like a performativity of the second class. There is first of all that primary performativity by means of which Christ enabled his word to do what it meant. Then there is a sacramental performativity by virtue of which the celebrant, in repeating those words in the context of the prayer of the Canon, so to speak restores to them their primary performativity. Of course mere linguistic analysis does not suffice to reveal this kind of performativity. Only the discernment of faith can recognize in this repetition the re-effectuation of the eucharistic mystery as the Apostles were enabled to experience it at the time of its institution, as it was presented originally to them in their faith at that time.

The present time in which liturgical language speaks is a moment between a grounding event (which it re-actualizes) and a horizon of realization which it anticipates. It is not the resumption of that which has already taken place and the announcement of that which is still awaited. The time to which liturgical language refers therefore has an eschatological structure. A more detailed analysis would have to try to reveal the action of this structure in the internal organization of liturgical language. Only thus could one show in what way it really "makes present" that which it talks of. It is ultimately its registration in an eschatological perspective which allows it its characteristic performativity.

But it is only the faith which impels it that gives it this reference to that which endows it with performativity. This faith gives the real orientation to the "Thou" to which the prayers are addressed and transforms a recitative language into a sacramental language, making the "Credo" a proclamation of that which it confirms. Yet faith is not an experience, silent in itself, which it is the function of liturgical language to describe. Between faith and liturgical language there is a kind of dual assumption. Faith takes up this language and gives it its own efficacy, inasmuch as faith is a resumption of the mystery of Christ, the acceptance of salvation and hope of benefits yet to come. Language is to faith a kind of structuring field which allows it to express itself in accordance with the exigencies of the reality to which it corresponds. This language is proclamation of the very content in which the faith is truly embodied, and is a sacramental accomplishment of the mystery which is thus announced and witnessed. Its threefold performativity enables faith to be expressed. This is ultimately due to the nature of faith, which is the hearing of the Word and the effective action of that Word in the actuality of a human life. If faith is the reception of the Word and if liturgical language receives from faith its characteristic performativity, that language is itself an echo of the Word. In the celebration it is the Word to which faith allows access that becomes present and operative in our own words. The Word became flesh and dwelt among us. Liturgical language is the location of his presence for us in the present day of celebration. It is from the Word that liturgical language receives the efficacy by virtue of which it becomes operative and makes effectively present that which it allows to appear in the area of its meanings. In so far as in and by faith we become participants in the mystery of the incarnation, our speech acts, in the liturgy, become the present mainstay of the manifestation of the Word. The basis of the performativity of liturgical language is the very mystery of this manifestation, which it celebrates and brings to pass.

Translated by John Griffiths

(c) *Addressing God in Faith*

Langdon Gilkey

I. How is the Holy present in our Worship?

THERE are many ways in which what we call "the contemporary crisis of faith" manifests itself. Most fundamental of all, it seems to me, is the elusiveness for all of us in our time of the holy, the absence for countless persons of a vivid sense of the presence of the divine—an absence felt not only in our daily life in the world but (even more devastating) an absence brought from the world into our holy places and experienced when Christians gather together in worship. This absence of deity in our common worship contributes to and even founds our other religious and theological problems. Were the presence of God real for us at least there, contemporary problems of belief or of God-language would be minimal, matters only of translation into current worldly modes of validation and of common "ordinary" forms of discourse. That on the contrary questions of the possibility of belief and of the meaningfulness of language about God are deep and significant issues even for the worshipping community—as they surely are—indicates, therefore, that at the heart of that community's life, in its common worship, there is experienced a compelling absence; for affirmation in faith of the reality of God and discourse about him alike depend upon an experience of his living presence. Thus the reality of common worship is the centre on which depend both Christian religious existence and Christian theology. We cannot evoke that reality by theological reflection —for, as with proofs of God, the dependency runs the other way —but, in such reflection we know, we move not towards the periphery of our ultimate concerns in theology but closer to their source and ground.

If there be, as I believe there are, problems in Christian worship peculiar to our age as well as those common to all periods, these former problems stem from the cultural or historical world that permeates us and that we bring with us into church. More of modernity than loud-speakers, sophisticated lighting and airconditioning inhabits our places of worship. The people who there listen, kneel and search for the divine presence in word and sacrament are also "modern", suffused with a secular consciousness that has tended to dissolve the sense of the holy wherever that consciousness has become dominant. Thus the words they hear communicate to them more about their clerical leader and his notions than about the Divine Word; the elements they receive are for many, if not most, merely signs of traditional sacralities, not living symbols of the divine presence; and what experiences they enjoy are for them at best their own subjective reactions and not the workings of the Holy Spirit.[1] The holy has appeared in the history of Christian worship in a variety of forms as sacrament, as Word, as spiritual possession. In each case the holy has not appeared alone or directly, but through the medium of something earthly—elements, speech and feelings. Now, even though the cultural reasons for its contemporary absence from these traditional media of the holy may not be consciously known or reflectively pondered (for example, a historical view of all words, even sacred ones, or a psychological view of all inner experiences), still the absence of the transcendent in and through these media is universally *felt* and therefore our worship is a problem.

For worship is not a self-generated activity; it is rather a response to the presence of the holy objectively experienced in our midst. It is not something that can be created or even evoked by us; as in revelation, it is *there* within its medium to be responded to (and that response is worship), or it is not there at all; hence if it is not there objectively for us, there can be no worship as response to its presence. Consequently, as every liturgist, traditional or experimental, knows, it is impossible to "create a sense of worship" by changing bodily movements, words, lights or music; nor by merely refashioning our forms of worship can we "make worship real". It may well be important for the possibility of our human response that such changes in liturgy be made. But the prior and more fundamental problem of the

---

[1] The contemporary phenomena of pentecostal experiences ("speaking with tongues") seems to belie these remarks about modernity. For groups devoted to a firm sense of these sorts of workings of the Spirit flourish in many of our churches, Protestant and Catholic alike. Perhaps such groups show the dissolution of modernity as "secular" in the sense here described, as quite possibly the counter-culture also does. My guess is that they do not. Rather it seems to me that such groups are only *partly* dominated spiritually by modernity (as are fundamentalist Protestants), and that the eagerness with which they embrace "the Spirit" in these forms shows how divested of ultimacy and sacrality the rest of their world is. The usual response of their pastor or priest (of incomprehension, grudging admiration and helplessness) is the best sign (or consequence) of what I mean by "secularity" and so modernity. His objection is not that these "speakers" are not orthodox Catholic in their piety, but that, as a modern man, he simply cannot credit, or understand, or participate in, these experiences—though he can hardly deny their power!

presence of the holy is another matter, for neither the repetition of traditional usages nor the adoption of new ones will in itself bring *that* presence about.[2] All *we* can do is to free our forms and to increase their relevance so that they can communicate the holy to us. It is God's presence that evokes worship, not our doing of worship that brings forth God.

If this be so, reflection on the problem of worship, in so far as it can at all be of help, is driven in the first instance not so much to consider more appropriate forms of worship as to reconsider and reappropriate the modes of presence of the holy in our tradition, to ponder at its deepest level how God comes to us in our community and our faith, to explore the most fundamental question of theology: how *is* God related to man, and how does man's awareness of that divine presence arise and flourish? Thus the history of worship, the history of piety and the history of theology are distinct but not separate histories; each history in its own way reflects the varying modes of the divine presence. Whenever worship has been vital and strong, its forms, as well as those of piety and theology, have been shaped by some vivid mode of the divine presence—as, for example, Reformation worship reflected the same manifestation of the holy through the word that was also the centre of both Reformation religious life and its theology. Consideration of worship at the most fundamental level, then, is consideration of the presence of God to men; it involves, therefore, every basic theological doctrine concerning the activity of God on us, in us and on our world. By pondering the mystery of the presence of God in all our being and living, we may be able to open our minds and ourselves to more special and concentrated forms of awareness of that presence—for worship is the community together celebrating and responding to that presence. In the following, therefore, we shall (in a very preliminary and inexpert

[2] This problem is in this sense similar to that of God-language. It is important that old, anachronistic forms of theological discourse be abandoned simply because they have become meaningless and so irrelevant to us; but the introduction of new forms does not in itself guarantee the ability to speak meaningfully about God. It is, so to speak, a necessary but not a sufficient condition, the deeper issue again being a sense of the holy or sacred as the prior condition for the meaningfulness of *any* form of theology.

way) try to think out the character of Christian worship at this fundamental level in the light of our theological understanding of the presence of God in human experience.

II. How is the Holy experienced in Christian Existence?

This question can be put more objectively as how does God relate himself to man in Christian faith? This dual question may well form the most fundamental question in theology; it surely does when we try to think out the theological foundations for worship. We shall here consider this question both formally and materially, with regard to the forms of our experience of the holy, and with regard to its matter, or more specifically, to the levels of our life in which this experience manifests itself. Such an examination may re-relate the modes of Christian worship to our real experiences of sacrality and thus, in reminding us of the continual presence of the holy in our existence, open us to its concentrated presence in communal worship.

We do not experience God directly in this life.[3] We are immersed in the creaturely and historical world God has created, and if we are aware of his presence at all, it is in and through his activity in that world, in and through what we call nature, history and its events, and our fellow men and ourselves. Thus is the presence of God always in a manner "hidden"—hidden within a finite medium which at once maintains its own creaturely integrity, powers, possibilities and weaknesses, and yet manifesting within itself the presence and activity of the divine. This fundamental pattern of divine presence within the creaturely is most universally expressed in the notion of creation: each en-

---

[3] As is evident, these statements imply that to me the mystical mode is a special vocation or gift within the Christian community and not normative for it. For most of us God comes to us, if at all, through finite media and not directly, that is *in* life and history and not beyond them. This appearance of the divine in and through the creaturely and the historical seems to me normative for the Christian tradition and so for its main forms of worship. Here I seem to be in some disagreement with my friend Louis Dupré, cf. his interesting book *The Other Dimension* (Garden City, 1972), esp. Chapter 12. Incidentally, this Thomist principle, in the modern context at least, in which thought is intrinsically confined to experience, means that theology can only speak of God in his relation to us, and not as he is in himself.

tity is and continues to be in its integrity and autonomy because of the divine activity in it of creation and preservation. It is further expressed in the doctrine of providence: the patterns of historical change brought about by creaturely action manifest as well the activity and so the purposes of God. But this "sacramental" or "theonomous" principle reaches its strongest and clearest expression in the incarnation: the presence of God for Christian faith is paradigmatically seen in the fully human person of Jesus. In each case the sacred or divine is present in and through the finite; in turn the finite in becoming itself is a vehicle or medium for that inward grace. For the creature to understand itself and its destiny *truly* as finite, and so to achieve its own true or "natural" integrity and autonomy, is *so* to understand itself, namely as upheld, directed, called and healed by the divine power. In this sense one can say that nature in its true being is not separated from grace. On the contrary, each creature in its essential or natural being is a *symbol* of the presence of the holy, and it becomes its authentic self when the pattern of its life inwardly and outwardly reflects that created status and role.[4] But this divine presence, and so the role or status of the creature as "symbol", is hidden—hidden within the integrity of finitude itself and veiled by our alienation from the sacred source and ground of our life. In us all it must be reawakened and reappropriated by special manifestations of the sacred; as a race and as individuals we must be "twice-born" because we are separated by our common sin from our own essential natures and so from an awareness of and a life within that continuing divine presence. It is in these particular manifestations of the sacred that the different religious traditions find their religious or theological (as opposed to their historical or cultural) roots and differentia. Here arises, then, a *second* sense of the word symbol, namely those special and unique media through which a particular revelation of the ultimate and the

---

[4] For this reason, as the history of religions illustrates, *any* creature can become a vehicle for some revelation of the holy, and in turn revelation of some sort may be said to be universal in scope. Obviously much of the differences between religions stems from the vast differences in the media which are taken as essential clues to the divine that is present in *all* creatures.

sacred, universally present but universally obscured as well, is now manifested in a particular form to a historical community, and so through which that group becomes aware of its own status as symbol (in the first sense), as existing in and through the power of the divine. In our Christian tradition, the significant "symbols" in this second sense are the history of the community of Israel and the person of Jesus.

Finally, in each tradition—and surely especially in our own —this presence of the divine in and through special events and persons is communicated over time to the community founded upon that special presence. This communication over time is in turn achieved through "symbols" in a *third* sense of that word. Again finite entities have become media which point to, recall and reintroduce by representation the originating presence of the holy in the "symbols" creative of that tradition. Such tertiary symbols are infinitely various in religion; in our tradition they are most importantly composed of communal acts and elements (sacraments) on the one hand, and spoken and reflected words on the other (kerygma, didache and the theological "symbols" which further reflection draws from them such as creation, providence, incarnation, atonement, etc.). Both (sacrament and word) are essential if our theological understanding of the divine presence is correct. Ultimacy is present in our living and being human, in the totality of our existence, not just to our minds and consciences. This *ontological* presence of the holy can be brought to awareness and recommunicated to us only through media which are as we are, and which analogically also communicate our being to us: water, bread and wine. On the other hand, the presence of the holy is hidden in the finite, that is, in ourselves and in these special media. Its presence must be evoked for us by a word that penetrates through the creaturely vehicle to the transcendent that appears within it and so a word that brings that transcendent dimension to our personal awareness, whether it be the transcendent at work in an historical event, in a sacramental element, or in our own existence.[5] Sacrament and word, ontological presence and kerygma, are essentially and yet dialec-

[5] This is only one of the bases for the presence of Word as well as sacrament in Christian existence; others will appear subsequently in our discussion.

tically interrelated in communicating the divine presence; this dialectical interrelation of the ontological and the personal or reflective levels will deepen as we proceed.

In turn our awareness of and response to the presence of the sacred—which is the heart of the problem of worship as response to the holy—combines these three senses of the word symbol. All Christian worship points to and finds its centre in the events or "symbols" originative of that tradition, to the Word in prophecy and the Word made flesh. Correspondingly the role of the tertiary symbols is to accomplish that pointing and center- ing, the sacraments of baptism and Eucharist with all of their manifold symbolic power re-presenting to us and in us these originating events, and the kerygma or proclamation opening up to us the transcendent meaning of those events and so calling us to decision and commitment in relation to them. The classical forms of Christian worship, Catholic and Protestant, have em- phasized—and often over-emphasized to the exclusion of the other—one or the other of these two forms of tertiary symbol. Certainly a more inclusive reinterpretation of both media is essential to the renewal of each of these two forms of Christian communion.

I suspect, however, that the present weakness of both classical forms of Christian worship lies not so much in this over- emphasis as in their common indifference to the first meaning of "symbol" as we delineated it, namely that the divine works in and on *us* as creatures too, and that awareness of this *our* role as "symbols"—in our being, our meanings, our decisions and our hopes—lies at the heart of any experience of the holy that is to be relevant to and effective in us. Put in terms of the history of ecclesiology, this may be called a plea for a renewed "spiritu- alist" principle in worship in which the relation in awareness of worshipper to God is primary; or in terms of contemporary philosophy, a plea for an "existential" relation on our part to sacrament and word alike. In terms of our previous theological discussion here and elsewhere, our argument is that unless the symbols of our tradition in word and sacrament are brought into relation to the ultimacy that permeates our ordinary life— unless traditional symbols reawaken in us our role as symbols of the divine activity—there is no experience of the holy. Sacramental and kerygmatic symbols remain meaningless and ineffective unless they communicate the holy to us, and that means unless they bring to our awareness the presence of the holy throughout the total character of our own existence. Thus in a secular age when ordinary life is separated in its self-understanding from its own transcendent ground, sacramental symbols unrelated to the transcendent dimension of our own existence in life become magical or merely traditional, and kerygmatic symbols change into empty theologisms or anachronistic signs of our moral and intellectual autonomy. The worship that responds to the Christian presentation of the holy in word and sacrament must be so related to lived experience that these traditional symbols communicate to us an awareness of our own essential relation to the holy. In order to be alive, religious symbols must provide shape and thematization to the patterns of ordinary life; correspondingly, natural, "secular" life must receive its fundamental forms from these symbols if it is to achieve its own essential goodness. God is already there in our existence as its ultimate ground and its ultimate goal. The role of sacrament and word alike is not so much to create or insert that presence into nature but to bring that prior relation forth in awareness and to give it the shape, power and form of Jesus Christ. The clue to renewed worship, as of a renewed Christian existence and theology, in so far as by reflection we can take hold of these matters, is to reappropriate through the forms of Christian symbolism the presence of the holy in the totality of ordinary existence.

III. How are we the Symbols of the Presence of God?

If the goal of worship is to reawaken through concentrated expression (an expression formed by Jesus Christ) our awareness of the ultimacy that forms the ground of and permeates our entire existence, then possibly our next question concerns the ways the holy manifests itself in our existence—*how* is it that we too are "symbols" of the presence of the divine activity?[6] For relevant,

[6] Generally discussions of "legitimate" worship have approached this interrelationship from the other side, namely by asking "What forms of worship are in fact 'genuine expressions' of Jesus Christ?" That is to say, they have asked for "valid" forms of sacrament and word. Since I think that this question, while important, is not the most helpful clue to our

meaningful and effective modes of worship will be those which, besides being faithfully "Christian", bring to awareness the modes of our own participation in and relation to the holy. Our discussion of the modes of manifestation of the holy in the totality of our existence may well in addition provide insight into both the perennial questions concerning our understanding of God and the perennial problems about the interrelation of the ontological and the moral, the impersonal and the personal in worship.

If God, as Christians believe, is the source and ground of our whole being, then the holy is crucially present on every level of our existence, providing the basis for every one of our essential or "ontological" powers. This active presence of ultimacy, giving our human nature its possibility and its form, may not be an aspect of our direct awareness, though, as we have argued elsewhere,[7] we all have as humans a subliminal awareness of the ultimate dimension in which we live. Still, this *is* the way we are related to God, and thus any sense in worship of the presence of God, while evoked for us by the symbols of our specific Christian tradition, will also be in part formed by the ways God works in and through us in our ordinary being and living.

There are many levels to our existence; and there are innumerable ways in which these different levels can be discriminated and named. Basic to all is the level of our being as such, our existence and life. Contingent, partial and transitory as it is, our finite being is the ground of all our activities and values and thus on every score of ultimate concern to us. We experience ultimacy initially in relation to the question of our being and our not-being as contingent creatures; thus an awareness of the holy is, or can be, communicated to us through our celebration of the gift of our own being. Through apprehension of the creation of

---

present problems of worship, but rather that the relations of even "valid" forms to ordinary, secular experience is the heart of the problem, we shall attack this difficult fortress, so to speak, from the rear, and explore the modes of the appearance of the holy in ordinary experience.

[7] For a fuller discussion of the dependence of all levels of our "nature" on the presence of the divine ultimacy, and the character of our "awareness" in ordinary life of this dimension of our existence, cf. the author's *Naming the Whirlwind: The Renewal of God-Language* (Indianapolis, 1969), Part II, Chapters 3 and 4.

our contingent being, we can be personally aware of the lived meaning of the symbol of creation and thus of the presence of the holy on that ontological level. Secondly, fundamental to our sense of worth or meaning in what we are and do is a context of ultimate meanings within which we act. This ultimate context of relations, social and historical, spanning past, present and future, is as necessary to our human being as is our existence; and so awareness of this context as expressive of the divine ultimacy is a second way of apprehending the holy as it manifests itself to us, a manifestation expressed symbolically in God's providential judgment and care over us and over our history. Again, when as rational beings we seek to understand and to know ourselves and our world, we also encounter ultimacy and sacrality under the form of truth. In apprehending this ultimacy in our ordinary existence, we may be able to apprehend the presence of the holy in worship under the Christians symbols of the divine Logos and the divine Truth. Finally, as autonomous beings we encounter the sacred as moral norm and so as obligation and responsibility, probably our first and most direct touch with deity in our developing experience. Following on this experience of the sacred as norm, the holy stands in our fallen existence over against us as condemnation, guilt and alienation; and we seek for renewal, self-acceptance and reconciliation. A plethora of Christian symbols correspond to and answer these "secular" experiences of conscience and judgment and the search for reconciliation which they inspire: law, wrath and grace. These are all quite ordinary experiences suffusing our daily existence; they stem from and point to ultimacy as it works in and on our being. To bring this ultimacy in its forms alike as existence and meaning, as norm, wrath, and grace, which is God, to awareness and to commitment as it is known in Christ, is to experience "faith", and to respond to that ultimacy so apprehended in and through these Christian symbols and so in the form of Jesus Christ, is to worship God. Word and sacrament provide the symbols by which this encounter with the holy is shaped and restored; but it is the

---

[8] A defence of this "Augustinian" viewpoint vis-à-vis knowledge and truth in terms of modern scientific inquiry is found in the author's *Religion and the Scientific Future* (New York, 1970), Chapter 2.

holy as it founds, permeates and restores our daily being that gives life, reality and meaning to these symbols and which provides the *presence* to which in worship we respond.

Essential to the view here expressed is the affirmation of a parallelism or correlation, as well as a crucial distinction, between the workings of the holy in and on us in our daily "secular" life and the deeper meanings of the Christian symbols or doctrines and so between general and special revelation, nature and grace, God as creative providence and God as redeemer. In this way the symbols (in senses 2 and 3) of our faith manifest to us our own status and role as by nature symbols (in sense 1) or creatures. And similarly our ordinary experience, apprehended in its ultimate dimension, gives to our Christian worship its life, relevance and power. Also essential to this view is the affirmation that while grace in and through Jesus Christ (what we have called a secondary level of symbol) brings something radically new and utterly unmerited into our ordinary existence, it does so only because of our fallen state, our separation from God and from our own natures in the exclusively autonomous rather than theonomous character of our existence. It is not to make up for a lack in our created nature that the unmerited and surprising grace communicated to us by the special revelation in Jesus Christ comes to us, but to overcome the distortion we have made in our natures and so in our history. Redemption fulfils creation; it does not transform it into something else or even something "higher", as if to fulfil our created human natures were not a high enough goal for a human existence, and as if that human goal did not have its own genuine glory in being at one and the same time a creative creature and also a "symbol" of the divine activity in history. But we must add that in refashioning our human being into its own created structure and purpose as such a "symbol", grace also thereby projects us into a *new* future—of ourselves and of history—which itself has a goal far beyond that of a mere repetition or even a restoration of the temporal past. Directedness towards an eschatological goal is the essential nature of both divine and human being, and so again grace in no way transcends nature but rather makes its realization and fulfilment possible.

If this analysis is correct, several conclusions follow about God and our relation in worship to him. The first is the multiplicity

of categories involved in God's relation to us, categories ontological and moral, impersonal and personal—a fact which
should warn us against an overemphasis on either the ontological
or the purely personal in understanding God or in structuring
worship (as Catholics and Protestants are both wont to do). This
plethora of categories appears, so to speak, twice. First because
the holy works in and on us, and thus can manifest itself to us,
on *all* levels of our existence from the level of our being or existence itself right up to the level of our rational and moral
autonomy, that is, from the impersonal organic base of our life
to its personal heights. Secondly, on each of these levels there is
a dialectic between an active divine presence that is *there* whether
we are personally aware of it or not (expressed, for example, in
the symbols of the divine creation, providence, judgment and care),
and our personal apprehension of and response to that presence.
As we have argued, an integration of this continual "ontological"
presence of the holy with our own personal apprehension of and
response to it is the heart of worship. Thus again our understanding of our relation to God and our participation in that relation in worship span ontological and moral, unconscious and
reflective, impersonal and personal categories. God is both "in"
us ontologically as an ultimate power of which we become aware,
and over against us as a "person" whom we encounter in moral
obligation and religious commitment, and so whom we can
address in dialogue. Neither set of categories can be used exclusively or univocally in theology or in worship. It is no arbitrary accident, then, that full worship—as full theological reflection—includes ontological, intentional, moral and personal levels,
and that in the case of each of these levels, sacramental presence
and personal word require each other. Without the element of
sacramental presence a form of worship composed only of reflective and moral concepts (as in liberal Protestantism) omits celebration of the divine ground of our fundamental being and our
deepest meanings, the ontological context within which we think
and act, and thus tends to dissipate its religious dimension into a
celebration of our personal autonomy. On the other hand, without the continual presence of *word* making possible personal reflection, decision, appropriation and commitment, the element of
sacramental presence fails to reach our personal being and thus

tends to be reduced to a mere traditionalism that can border on the rote and even the magical.

A second implication of this understanding of the holy and its presence to us in and through symbols gives the basis for the social or communal character of worship. The secondary and tertiary symbols through which the holy is reawakened and re-appropriated (originating revelation and its symbolic witness in sacrament and word) come to us in history through a tradition, that is through a community structured by these symbols. In this community and through these symbols the holy that permeates our ordinary life has come to our awareness, and in faith our life is now grounded, directed, called and healed. Thus our own ex-perience of the holy—and so our worshipping response to it—is essentially communal in its origin and its actualization; it is not and cannot be something that we do alone merely as individuals either in time or in space. Secondly, man as man is both on-tologically and personally communal. Our existence and life, our personal being, the possibility and modes of our speech, our re-flections and our activities come to us from community and take the forms of our own communal origin. We cannot *be* as human beings without society. Thus any apprehension of the ultimate mystery that founds and upholds our human being inevitably culminates in a social apprehension, for it is as "fellow men" and not as individuals that we are there and there as human. Thirdly, Christian man is social and communal—he celebrates his creation through the life and love of other human beings, and he is called by the Gospel to minister to others if he is to be whole. He arises out of love both human and divine, and he is sent forward into love and community as the deepest personal meaning of his human being. On every ground, then, man's relation to the divine is both personal and social; as the ontological and the per-sonal levels interpenetrate in worship at every level, so no in-dividual man, and especially no Christian man, can apprehend, celebrate or obey the holy except in community.

Finally, if this be so, worship has an historical and ultimately an eschatological *telos* and fundamental meaning. Because we are ontologically and morally communal beings, made from and for each other; and because we exist in time so that *what* we are, ontologically and morally, is a projection forward towards an end, therefore the holy in its creative, providential, normative and redemptive work on us moves us away from ourselves outward into history and forward into the future. This ontological fact about our being receives its fullest symbolic expression in the Kingdom to which we are called in this life and beyond it in eternity, and whose coming is the key to understanding the divine intentionality structuring all we can know of the holy. The divine ultimacy that founds and upholds us in the present, and that calls us out into the social and historical world and forward into that world's future, is itself directed forward to its own divine goal. Our apprehension of God and our response to him, therefore (like our apprehension of and actualization of ourselves and our history), are temporal and eschatological, directed into a future whose mystery remains but whose ultimate shape is to be determined by the same love and power that in our Christian present has already established us.

Irénée-Henri Dalmais

The Expression of the Faith
in the Eastern Liturgies

AN unfortunate dissociation has developed in the "Western" Christian churches of the Latin tradition between an academic theology spread by catechism teaching and a sentimental or moralistic pietism which grew up alongside a liturgy artificially preserved and restored under the influence of the clergy. This split has produced enormous difficulties which threaten the success of the liturgical renewal set in motion by Vatican II.

Christians of the "Eastern" traditions, on the other hand, find it hard to understand why this reform should mean an abrupt break with rites and formulas inherited from a long tradition, which, in spite of having become impoverished and ossified, goes back without any major break to the heart of the ecclesial life of the first communities. The structure of this life was also in large part a continuation of the forms and expressions of the prayer of the synagogue, so full of biblical reminiscences, which Gentile converts to Christianity had assimilated from the beginning. It should be recognized, however, that the liturgy of the Roman Church, which was to form the core of the liturgical expression common to all the Latin West, was very different, in the style of its formulas and the extreme sobriety of its ritual, from what could be called the ecumenical pattern to be found in the various Eastern liturgies and also to a large extent in the old Latin liturgies, the Milanese, the Spanish and the Gallican.

It is clearly valuable, in the current search for a new language of faith, especially in the privileged area of its liturgical expression, to examine this tradition, and to note the various forms it has taken in the various cultures enshrined in the liturgical expression of the different "Rites".[1] This common stock seems to have been formed for the most part in Syria–Palestine, and more precisely in Antioch. This cosmopolitan city was a meeting place, not only for a very large and active Jewish community, but also for representatives of other Semitic cultures—notably the one which originated in the Christian centre of Edessa (Urfa) in Upper Mesopotamia—in close contact with the Christian communities beyond the Euphrates and those influenced by Graeco–Roman culture. Antioch was also, of course, an important centre of Hellenistic culture; the church of Antioch accepted expressions of faith produced in the communities of Anatolia, especially in Cappadocia when, in the second half of the fourth century, the "Cappadocian Fathers" (Basil, Gregory of Nyssa and Gregory Nazianzen) made the province one of the most important centres for the ecclesial expression of the faith. The whole of this rich inheritance was to spread to the farthest outposts of the Christian world, both East and West, in the admirably popular and practical form which it acquired in the celebrations at the holy places in Jerusalem and which were brought back by the first pilgrims.[2] But Antioch also had an influence of its own, which was particularly strong in Egypt and Ethiopia. More than any other liturgy, that of Antioch was the model for the liturgy of Constantinople and consequently for the Byzantine rite which was the result of the coming together of the traditions of Constantinople, Antioch and Palestine. This rite became the common liturgy of the Orthodox churches and is often taken for the sole expression of the Eastern liturgical tradition.

Out of the vast treasury of formulas and rites contained in this tradition, we can only consider here those elements which in my view are both the most important and the most relevant to our own present interests.

[1] This term, whose meaning has always been rather vague, is used here in its canonical and liturgical sense of a liturgical expression of the faith transmitted within the framework of an autonomous ecclesiastical structure. See Antoine Joubeir, *La notion canonique de Rite* (Rome, 1961).

[2] We know them mainly through the "Journal of Etheria" (or Egeria), written by a pilgrim towards the end of the fourth century (probably 381–384), and also from the Lectionary preserved in an Armenian translation (ed. A. Renoux, *Patres Orientales*, pp. 163 and 168).

I. Proclaiming the Name of God and Manifesting his Glory

It is fitting that every mouth should glorify, every voice confess, every creature venerate and proclaim the adorable and glorious name (of the most holy Trinity, the Father, Son and Holy Spirit)[3] which created the world in its grace and the peoples in its mercy, saved men in its compassion and gave mortals so great a blessing. . . .

These first words of the very old eucharistic prayer "of the Apostles", still in use in the Nestorian, Chaldean and Syro-Malabar churches, brings down to our time the tradition of the Aramaic-speaking communities, which is in direct continuity with the forms of prayer in the synagogue. In this tradition, this privileged form of the "blessing" (*berakah*) is regarded as the most appropriate, if not the only proper, one for testifying to God whose secret being remains inaccessible but whose name has been revealed by the works of the Son and the manifestations of the Spirit. That is why the prayer continues by mentioning *"the immeasurable grace which we can never repay. You took on our humanity. You came down to us with your divinity. You raised us up from our fallen state, revived our mortal flesh. . . ."*

A very old Jewish-Christian prayer of thanksgiving preserved in Greek in Book VII of the *Apostolic Constitutions*,[4] which can be shown to have influenced the most characteristic expressions of the Antiochene liturgy preserved in the Byzantine rite, multiplies adjectives which by their negative form preserve the transcendent and unutterable character of the mystery of God. At a very early stage, in the face of the rigorous rationalism which was to cause serious disruption in the life of the Church in the Greek world during the Arian crisis, it was felt necessary to give great emphasis—particularly in the celebrations of the liturgy—to the fact that God could not be known as well as to his manifestation in creation and the history of salvation which was completed and fulfilled in Christ. Many expressions inherited from

---

[3] This trinitarian expression of faith was probably introduced after the fourth century.

[4] Attention was drawn to it by W. Bousset, *Nachrichten von der k. Gesellschaft der Wissenschaften zu Göttingen* (1915), pp. 435–85 and E. R. Goodenough, *By Light, Light* (New Haven, Conn., 1935), chap. 11.

Hellenistic Judaism were readily available for this purpose. At the same time, however, it was necessary to stress the divinity of Christ, equal in all things to the Father, which was consecrated by the Council of Nicaea by the technical term *homoousios* (consubstantial). This term itself was to become part of liturgical language, perhaps even before the creed placed under the patronage of Nicaea became a profession of faith required of the faithful before they could take part in the celebration of the Eucharist. (The solemn character of this declaration was later underlined in the Byzantine liturgy by the order for vigilance addressed to the deacons: "The doors, the doors!")

More easily intelligible formulas and rites were sought, however, for the majority of believers, and it seems almost certain that it is in this context that we should place the introduction, at the very beginning of the liturgy, of the *trisagion* acclamation found in all the Eastern liturgies: "Holy God, mighty God, immortal God, have mercy on us." It is certainly the Byzantine rite which emphasizes most strongly the transcendence and the unknowable aspect of God. In addition to the prayers recited by the celebrant during the singing of the *trisagion*, we may mention the anthem sung during the procession which accompanies the bread and wine destined for the celebration of the Eucharist through the church to the sanctuary (the Grand Entry): *"Let us, who hear in mystery the icon of the cherubim and sing the thrice-holy hymn to the life-giving Trinity, put aside all the cares of the world to welcome the king of the universe, escorted invisibly by the angelic armies. Alleluia."* Here again the prayer of the priest which precedes this anthem stresses the awe-inspiring character of the theophany symbolized by this ceremony. The Byzantine liturgy has only one variant of the hymn of the cherubim reserved for the Easter vigil, but the Armenian liturgy has a variety of texts which all express the same idea.

That idea is to create the atmosphere of a theophany, because it is in Christ, and only in him, that the inaccessible secret of divine transcendence has been revealed. Admittedly, a reflection may also be seen in creation, as is proclaimed by the anaphora of St James, the eucharistic prayer of the Church of Jerusalem which has had a considerable influence on various Eastern liturgies: *"The heavens, the heavens, the heavens, all the heavenly armies, the sun, the moon and the millions of stars, the earth and the sea and all that they contain, the heavenly Jerusalem, the church of the firstborn whose names are written in heaven, the angels . . ."* sing the praise of the most holy God.

This mystery was revealed gradually in the course of the history of salvation, and the main stages of that history are mentioned in the various eucharistic prayers, especially those of St James and St Basil which are in use in many liturgies. But, both in the celebration of the Eucharist and in the course of the instruction of catechumens, faith in Christ as the only revelation of divine glory is constantly stressed. The christological controversies which prolonged the Arian crisis for more than two centuries and created lasting divisions in several Eastern churches stimulated a rich profusion of texts which, in a variety of languages and cultures, attempt to preserve the Orthodox faith. Only the archaic Aramaic liturgy of the Mesopotamian communities, which were separated from the rest of the Christian world at a very early date by their political position within the Sassanid Persian empire, has kept an acclamation which may very well go back to the earliest Jewish-Christian communities: *"To you, Lord* (Lakumara) *of the universe, go our praises, to you, Jesus Christ, our blessings; you are the one who gives life to our bodies, you are the saviour of our souls."* In all the other liturgies this has been replaced, probably during the sixth century, by an anthem which the Byzantine tradition ascribes to the Emperor Justinian and which may well be the work of Severus of Antioch, or may at least have been introduced by him into the Sunday liturgy; only the Coptic rite keeps it for a few particularly solemn celebrations: *"O only begotten son* (Monogenēs) *and Word of the Father, you who, being immortal, were willing to become incarnate in the womb of the holy mother of God, the ever-virgin Mary, to save us; you who, without change, became man and were crucified; Christ our God, by your death you conquered death; you who are one of the holy Trinity, glorified with the Father and the Holy Spirit, save us."* It is remarkable that the churches which were faithful to the Chalcedonian orthodoxy, so careful to avoid anything which they saw as having the slightest taint of Monophysitism, seem to have had no reluctance to adopt such a text. The reason is that they—like the whole Eastern Christian tradition—felt it essential to make quite clear and to instil into their members their faith in the divinity of Christ in whom the inaccessible mystery of God was manifested for us.

In order to express as vividly as possible the paradox of the Christian faith, the liturgical tradition which derived from Antioch and Jerusalem frequently made use of antitheses which contrast the unchanging glory of the creative Word with the humiliations of the incarnation and passion. The following example is from Good Friday vespers in the Byzantine rite: *"On this day we see enacted a terrible and extraordinary mystery: the intangible ceases; he who released Adam from the curse is chained; he who searches hearts is subjected to an unjust investigation; he who sealed the abyss is sealed in prison; they bring before Pilate him before whom the powers of heaven tremble; they beat the maker of creation; the judge of the living and the dead is condemned to the gallows; he who sacked hell is placed in a tomb. Lord, so patient, you who suffer everything for love, who save men from the curse, glory to you."*

II. The Liturgy as Play and Poem

Texts like these come from a form of liturgical expression which is relatively rare in the Western Roman tradition. The Roman tradition has forged euchological formulas of admirable brevity and of a density which makes any translation or even any adaptation impossible. We must recognize that in contrast the euchology of the Eastern liturgies in the strict sense contains, apart from the eucharistic prayers (*anaphoras*), only a few texts which can stand comparison. We must look elsewhere and to other forms for the genius of these traditions. Their spirit is much more concrete and poetic, and prefers to move in the sphere of the imagination. The liturgical celebration in these traditions takes the form of a great community game, activating all the powers of the imagination and sensibility which can induce an experience of the active presence of the Spirit who comes to complete the mystery of salvation in the Church. This is the reason for the role and the importance given to the prayer for the coming of the Spirit (the *epiclesis*). The degree of incomprehension shown for so long in this respect by Latin theologians, particularly as regards the role of the *epiclesis* in the celebration of the Eucharist, is well known. In the Syrian tradition the importance of this moment is highlighted on the occasion of all the great consecrations considered as sacramental: that of baptismal water, of the scented oil of chrism (*myron*), of the eucharistic bread and wine. On each occasion, as the celebrant bows down to beg for the coming of the Spirit, the deacon proclaims: *"My dear friends, how terrible and solemn is this moment, the moment when the Holy Spirit comes from the sublime world of heaven, descends on this offering and consecrates it. Watch and pray in silence and fear. Pray."*[5]

As an introduction to this sacred time and in order to show its full meaning, the various Eastern liturgies have drawn in the first place on the wealth of ideas and images contained in the Bible, and they have also used the great cosmic symbols. Faith in Christ as the fulfilment of the messianic hope, setting the seal on the work of creation and inaugurating the eschatological fullness, has been expressed through this play of images and symbols. And it is once more in Syria–Palestine that this rich poetic *corpus* on which all the Eastern liturgies have drawn first took shape. Apart from the arrangement of readings and the singing of psalms and biblical chants which form the indestructible framework of any Christian liturgical expression, hymnography, euchology and homiletics fell into extremely flexible rhythms which it was easy to transpose into different languages. The liturgy of the hours and those of the eucharistic and sacramental celebrations, and all other religious functions, had only to draw on this, adapting the same common stock according to their needs and to the individual characteristics of their languages and cultures. The result is liturgies in the form of lengthy poems in which singing, movements and gestures, even religious art, especially in the Byzantine tradition, play as important a role as verbal expression. The latter, as is still most often the case, may continue to be formulated in an archaic language or even in one no longer used; the need of translation is hardly felt. The litur-

[5] On the role of the Holy Spirit in Syrian eschatology, see E. P. Siman, *L'expérience du saint-Esprit par l'Eglise d'après la tradition syrienne d'Antioche* (Paris, 1971).

gical action is lived; it is an experience as well as a profession of faith. A few gestures, a few formulas familiar to all are enough. In spite of the frequent richness of the doctrinal content of the texts, it is their character as witnesses to the faith of the Church more than their detailed meaning which is important in the liturgy.

III. The Eschatological Perspective

This attitude, which is surprising and even shocking to many Westerners formed by a predominantly conceptual culture and academic system, can only be properly understood if one keeps in mind, as well as the deep sense of the unknowability of God and the indescribable character of his mystery which was discussed earlier, the atmosphere of eschatological waiting which saturates the Eastern liturgies. The emphasis may be different according to the various cultures and historical situations within which the various liturgies have developed. The Byzantine tradition, and to a lesser degree the Armenian tradition which is close to it, concentrate above all on the anticipation of the manifestation of the eschatological kingdom contained in the liturgical celebration. In the well-known words of the Russian theologian Serge Bulgakov, the liturgy is "heaven on earth". That is why Christians formed in this tradition, and especially the Slavs, regard it as of first importance that the Church should be able to maintain the essentials of the liturgical life by which it proclaims and anticipates the kingdom which is to come and the victory won by Christ over the powers of evil and death. This attitude is expressed, for example, in the anthem at the "Grand Entry" which replaces the *Hymn of the Cherubim* at the Easter vigil: *"Let all flesh keep silence and remain in fear and trembling, and let it entertain no earthly thought. For the king of kings, the lord of lords, is coming forward to be sacrificed and to give himself as food for the faithful. The angelic choirs go before him with all the principalities and the powers. The Cherubim with their countless eyes and the Seraphim with their six wings cover their faces and sing, Alleluia, alleluia, alleluia."*

The emphasis is different in the strictly Syrian liturgies. These have continued to use the Syriac language, of which Louis Massignon said, "Syriac is the language of the incarnation in this

world which will be judged, the language of the particular examination, the language of fire, of the interior trial, the language
of the bearing of prisoners, of those mysterious things of penance,
fasting and alms, the sign of the greatest love, for to deprive
yourself for the one you love is to be already filled."[6] These
liturgies have been described as moving in a "purgatorial universe—theological moralizing about purification and an eschatological waiting for the glory of the *parousia* are their two main
themes".[7] Here the language is that of an endless vigil, which
never stops pondering on the biblical texts and their poetic commentary while waiting for the manifestation of the light which
is the subject of a famous hymn of the Chaldean and Maronite
liturgies, which attribute its authorship to the great Syrian doctor,
St Ephraem.

IV. CONCLUSION

In these few pages it has been impossible to do more than
mention briefly the subjects in the expression of the faith which
seem most typical of the Eastern liturgical traditions. They concern
what is most fundamental and most specific, the manifestation
of the inaccessible mystery of the triune God in the history of
salvation, the incarnation and the saving work of Christ, the time
of whose eschatological fulfilment by the gift of the Spirit has
been opened by the resurrection. To introduce the faithful—who
are the subjects of the Christian liturgy—to the experience of
these realities, the liturgy draws mainly, if not exclusively, on
reminiscences of Scripture as interpreted by the patristic tradition, without trying to adapt it to different periods or new situations. In other words, the Eastern liturgical traditions seem so
far to show no interest in the search for a new language of faith
because they regard the liturgy are pre-eminently the place where
each Christian is called to confront the tradition received from
the Fathers. This is perhaps one of the most important points in
the difficult dialogue which is beginning between East and
West.

[6] Lecture to the 1948 Conference of Carmelite Studies, "Techniques et
contemplation" (Beirut, 1964), p. 548.
[7] Michel Hayek, *Liturgie Maronite* (Paris, 1964), Introduction, p. xv.

Translated by Francis McDonagh

Casper Honders

Let us Confess our Sins . . .

I. Orientation

TO WRITE about various aspects of the confession of sin and guilt in communal worship[1] within the theme of the liturgical experience and expression of faith is no easy matter. Like any other author attempting to discuss this subject, I at once recognized that I had for a long time been pulled this way and that by the conflicting data and views that are current in this very polarized debate. What is more, I was conscious of the confusion, uncertainty and even existential shame that exists at present whenever the question of the confession of guilt within the framework of public worship and of faith arises.[2]

So much is, after all, involved, in terms of theology, ethics and social and political life, in this whole question, but in this article it is clear that we can do no more than make a preliminary reconnaissance of this enormous territory. We have to do this because the community of Christ has been called to express its faith, hope and love before God and man now and in the future and at the same time to confess openly how "broken-hearted" and "crushed in spirit" it is (see Ps. 34. 19; 51. 19),[3] in a con-

---

[1] Although a distinction should normally be made between "sin" and "guilt", I use these words indiscriminately here.

[2] In addition to the standard manuals and dictionaries on the liturgy, see also Paul Surlis, ed., *Faith: Studies in its Nature and Meaning* (Dublin), especially H. Berkhof's article on "The Reformation Concept of Faith and Its Development through History", which was first published in the *Nederlands Theologisch Tijdschrift* (Jan. 1972), pp. 32–46.

[3] I follow the Hebrew numbering of the psalms.

fession of guilt. As van Ruler has so correctly said: "The reality of evil means that man is either guilty or tragic. A choice has to be made between guilt and tragedy. It is possible to find oneself in the abyss of the tragic sense of life as the result of a 'mild' preaching of the Gospel which gives scant attention to the question of helping the sinner to discover himself. The man who overlooks guilt inevitably falls a victim to fate."[4]

The chief temptation for the liturgical specialist here is to turn from the question of guilt itself to the rubrics that apply to the confession of that guilt. The data which can be produced from the past and the present are usually quite clear. As a result, we have to remember that our confusion will increase, our uncertainty will become greater and our shame more acute. Once again, we shall come to realize how dangerously close we come to the very heart of the Christian community when we call for a confession of guilt, which is both a "postlude" and a "prelude". It is a "postlude" because the glory of God's name first exposes the darkness of our works and the vulnerable nature of our faith, with the consequence that we are bound to say that the confession of guilt always follows the proclamation of grace.[5] "The Old Testament also belongs to the canon precisely because it is said today in God's name that a man must have been touched by God's name and must share in the benefits of God's covenant if he complains, rebels and doubts as he does."[6] And this statement applies not only to the Old Testament, but also to the whole of the Church's testimony and to the public confession of guilt as well as to complaint, rebellion and doubt.

At the same time, however, this confession of guilt is also a "prelude" in so far as it is closely connected with the confident expectation of God's words of grace and the realization of his promises. For this reason, the confession of guilt always precedes

[4] A. A. van Ruler, *Waarom zou ik naar de kerk gaan?* (Nijkerk, n.d.), an excellent "liturgical" book which has so far not been translated into another European language.

[5] See K. Barth's comments relating to the liturgy in *Kirchliche Dogmatik*, iv, 3-2, pp. 1013 ff. and his broader treatment of God's judgment ("Gottes Gericht") and man's acquittal ("Des Menschen Freispruch") in *op. cit.*, iv, 1, pp. 589-678.

[6] K. H. Miskotte, *Als de goden zwijgen* (Amsterdam, 1956), p. 196.

the reading of Scripture, the sermon and the Lord's supper—
because of its decisive relationship with God's forgiveness and
grace, it has the character of dependence.

II. Questions

Within the context of the confusion, uncertainty and shame
to which I referred in the previous section, several questions
arise. The first and most important is, do we still agree that the
confession of guilt is directed towards and dependent on the
speaking and the presence of the God of Israel and the Father
of our Lord Jesus Christ? It is so often claimed today that he is
hidden, absent or dead or that he can only be called upon in a
given situation, or in social or political activity. "To insist on
the theme of God gives a sense of urgency to the question about
the meaning of the worship of God."[7]

A second and related question is, what does the testimony of
the Bible mean to us? If it has lost its meaning for us, what is
the purpose of continuing to point to it? In Jacob, Moses, David,
Job, Jeremiah, the penitential psalms, Lamentations, the prodigal
son, the publican and 1 John 1, the legal dispute between God
and his people should be made present for us. If it is not, is this
because we have been too triumphalist or one-sided in our interpretation of tradition, our "deposit of faith" or the culture in
which we live?[8]

A third and again related question is, to what extent do we
invite a confrontation with the law, the commandments and the
institutions of God in our confession of guilt? What will then
convince us of our sin and guilt? And how can guilt be made
public if not by the law which is spiritual and good? It cannot
be deduced from the position of the stars, the behaviour of
society, the individual or collective conscience or the laws of the
Church.

[7] Gerhard Ebeling, "Die Notwendigkeit des christlichen Gottesdienstes",
Zeitschrift für Theologie und Kirche, 2 (1970), p. 235.

[8] See, for example, Charles Davis' article, "Ghetto or Desert: Liturgy in
a Cultural Dilemma", in *Studia Liturgica*, 2 (1970), pp. 10–27, in which
the idea of "culture", or "Christian culture" in this case, is overstressed
and the future of Christian worship is conceived too narrowly.

III. THE DECALOGUE

In the traditional Sunday worship of both the Dutch Reformed and the Anglican churches, the decalogue acts as a framework for the confession of guilt. This is strikingly clear from the preparatory part of the Sunday service based on the sixteenth-century model of Valerandus Pollanus.[9] In this liturgy, the congregation, led by the cantor, began by singing verses 1 to 5 of a rhyming version of the ten commandments. (These first five verses corresponded to the first tablet of the Law.) After the president's "our help is in the name of the Lord" (Ps. 124. 8), the people publicly confessed that they were "poor sinners" who, because they had constantly transgressed against God's commandments and could not withstand his judgment, were sincerely repentant and appealed to his mercy "in the name of thy Son, Jesus Christ our Lord". They then declared that they relied on the Holy Spirit to renew them daily and to enable them to recognize their iniquities and to produce the fruits of justice and innocence which would please God through his Son Jesus Christ.[10] The one who was leading in worship would then read some scriptural words of forgiveness and pronounce, over those who had faith and repentance, the remission of sins "in the name of the Father, of the Son and of the Holy Ghost". After this, verses 6 to 8 (the second tablet of the Law) of the hymn based on the ten commandments were sung, at the conclusion of which the president led the congregation in prayer, asking God, who had given them the ten commandments through Moses, to inscribe his Law on their hearts through his Holy Spirit, because they longed only to serve and obey him in holiness and justice. This preparation for the Sunday service then concluded with the singing of the last verse of the hymn, which called for strength to obey God's will.

This preparation, which is, I believe, still very inspiring, is the prelude to a liturgical drama expressing judgment, forgiveness and renewal of the whole life of the believing community

[9] See my edition of *Valerandus Pollanus Liturgia sacra*, 1551-5 (Leyden, 1970), pp. 54-61.

[10] G. van der Leeuw has called this confession of guilt "the most beautiful and precious element in the whole liturgy of the reformed church".

by means of confrontation with God's will. I believe that this sixteenth-century communal confession of guilt can still be of great value to us today, although it would clearly have to be adapted to the different language and ideas of twentieth-century man and to the changed social and political structures. As believers, we still have to look to the evangelical decisions imposed on us here and now by God for solutions to social and political problems and we cannot do this unless we find a place in communal worship for the recognition of our sins, both as individuals and as a community, and for our absolution from them. When this happens, the masquerade of human and probably also of so-called "Christian" plans and structures becomes patently obvious. It is, however, important in this context to respect both the desire to remain an individual in faith and the need to renew and to criticize social and political structures as a believing community.[11]

IV. Changes and Transitions

It is valuable in this context to compare two confessions of guilt—the *Confiteor* of the Roman rite and the "Open Guilt" of the reformed tradition. Both are placed at the beginning of the liturgy as a kind of "up beat" and are very similar, however different they may be in language, character, function and intention. There is, for example, not only the "I" who confesses his sins—bearing in mind especially what he is called to do as an office-bearer—but also the communal confession of all those who will approach the Lord's table.

It is important, however, to note that very little is said in these confessions on which we can fasten. As soon as we try to grasp hold of one point as a definite act made by the Church, we become aware of constant changes. This is almost certainly because there is a continuous blurring of the dividing line between the liturgy and pastoral concern, because the Church and society are always influencing each other and because sins have to be fol-

[11] In connection with the confession of guilt, three questions have again and again in the history of the Church been asked of believers: 1. Do we acknowledge and confess our sins? 2. Do we believe in the redemption brought about by Jesus Christ? 3. Do we want to live in thankfulness and renewed obedience? These three closely related questions have always played an important part in the liturgy, the pastoral care and the catechetics of the Dutch reformed tradition.

lowed far beyond the walls of the church. As an example of this, if we think of the liturgical preparation for the Lord's Supper in the reformed churches, we at once encounter the roots of the practice of parish visiting. Again, the origin of liturgical confession of guilt is to be found, at least partly, in the behaviour and words of those who are in danger of succumbing to physical and spiritual temptations in the world. There are, then, frequent transitions in both directions between the individual and the community, the Church and the world, the liturgy and pastoral care, the office-bearer and the priesthood of all believers, the confession of guilt and political action. These changes, transitions and cases of interrelationship should not be obstructed. On the contrary, they are healthy and can stimulate the people of God to confess their guilt with a particular situation in mind.

V. The Bible and Liturgy

Again and again, the Church has returned to Scripture as the first source of liturgical material in the confession of guilt. It would be very instructive, for example, to investigate how psalms 6, 32, 51 and 130 have been incorporated at different times by various Christian denominations and in many forms into the liturgy—for instance, into prayers, hymns, the administration of baptism and the celebration of the Lord's Supper. In addition to the penitential psalms, there is the Old Testament as a whole, in which we are shown the condition and the conduct of the poor of Yahweh, their sufferings and complaints and their consciousness of guilt. "The so-called Old Testament forms part of the one Scripture, so that we may learn how to express and to confess our suffering to God in a fully human way."[12] There are also special and highly relevant passages in the Old Testament, such as Jer. 17 and Ezekiel 18.

As examples of the use of the New Testament in the confession of guilt, I would point only to the story of the prodigal son (Luke 15. 11–32, especially 15. 21), the pharisee and the publican (Luke 18. 9–14, especially 18. 13) and also to Rom. 7 and 1 Cor. 11 (especially 1 Cor. 11. 27–29 in the preparation for the Lord's Supper). Both the individual believer and the community are

[12] K. H. Miskotte, *op. cit.*, p. 67.

invited to an examination of conscience by exhortations based on and inspired by such passages. The Lord's Prayer (Matt. 6. 9–13), either as such or in paraphrase or else used as the basis for discourse or for instruction, has also been employed effectively both in the liturgy and in catechetics.

Finally, the appeal for mercy and forgiveness and the confession of sin and guilt have always been heard in the whole liturgy of the Catholic Church as well. The very fact of the people's participation in the services of the Church shows that they are ready to join the ranks of sinners seeking pardon. The temptations to which they are exposed in their contacts with the world and their fellow men are included, expressed and confessed in the Roman rite in the *Kyrie, the Gloria (Domine . . . Jesu Christe . . . qui tollis peccata mundi, misere nobis)*, the Creed (*Confiteor unum baptisma in remissionem peccatorum*) and the *Agnus Dei.*

VI. CHRISTIANS NOW

In 1973, Christianity is divided and its continued existence is seriously threatened. Do we confess our guilt for the part we have played in this phenomenon and do we use the confession of guilt as it were as our visiting card in our contact with the non-Christian world? In this, it is important to bear in mind that basing our approach to our non-Christian fellow men on the confession of guilt as a universally human phenomenon that will be recognized by all men might well lead to the wrong results. As a universally human phenomenon taking place in the world, the Christian confession of guilt is on the same level as being expelled from the party, dismissed from one's job and condemned to live anonymously and without status in society. As an action performed within the Christian community, on the other hand, it has a direct bearing on our relationship with the one God within the covenant. The God to whom we confess our sins within the community of faith gives us faith and gives us his Son, "who knew no sin" but whom God "made to be sin" for us "so that in him we might become the righteousness of God" (2 Cor. 5. 21). "Preaching and the liturgy are a disclosure which makes psychoanalysis fade into insignificance."[13]

[13] A. A. van Ruler, *op. cit.*, p. 67.

In the whole matter of giving a permanent place in church services to the confession of guilt and the proclamation of grace,
there are good theological, liturgical and pastoral reasons for referring this "rubric" back to preaching.[14] The very essence of the
Gospel is to be found where faith is given to the proclamation
of God's grace. The confession of guilt and the proclamation of
grace both have a strongly liturgical character—they are collective and repetitive and have a highly concentrated form of expression and a fixed structure. This fixed liturgical character may
have a harmful effect on preaching, which is of necessity more
free, subtle and colourful.

Finally, there is the hopeless, even impossible situation which
arises when the "new obedience" to which the Christian is called
after confessing his guilt turns out to be fictitious. We are bound
to ask ourselves whether the time may not come when the
strictly liturgical confession of guilt has not to be exposed as a
practice that lacks truth and conviction. Let me cite one example. If Christians continue to confess their guilt for the
divisions in the community of Christ while lacking the will to
reunite, does this not mean that the question of Christian reunion
has really lost credulity and that the liturgical confession has become purely automatic? We cannot and should not, "when we
hear the promises of the Gospel, leave the structure of faith and
repentance".[15] Disobedience cannot with impunity take the place
of obedience.

VII. Conclusion

I should like to conclude by suggesting a number of separate
confessions that could, I think, usefully be included in the liturgical confession of guilt as a whole:

(1) That we have behaved with idolatry, even superstitition,
in our slavish dedication to liturgical actions, formulas and laws,
so that our happiness in serving and loving the one God has
become impaired;

---

[14] J. T. Bakker has written a helpful article about this in the *Jaarboek
voor de Eredienst van de Nederlandse Hervormde Kerk* (1960), pp. 18-33,
entitled "Vragen rond de genadeverkondiging".

[15] J. T. Bakker, *op. cit.*, p. 30.

(2) that we have gone to such lengths to create an image of God's being in liturgical words and actions that we have built an obstacle to his inspiring Word and his encouraging Spirit;

(3) that we have sworn so often in the name of our liturgical traditions and our synodal decisions that we have obscured, abused and defamed God's name and made it difficult for us to call upon it;

(4) that we have treated the liturgical structures which have been given to us for use in church services and in catechetics like plunder that we ourselves have taken or like a worn-out garment to be discarded, thus spoiling for ourselves the taste of peace in God's sabbath;

(5) that we have given such authority and dignities to those bearing office and leading worship that we have diminished the effective power of God's will among men, Christ's rule over the world and the indwelling of the Holy Spirit in our hearts;

(6) that we have made it difficult for men to live freely and happily in God's presence by our liturgical casuistry and indifference;

(7) that we have not succeeded in overcoming the tensions in human society by our liturgical celebration of God's love and have thus impaired the effectiveness of the Gospel;

(8) that we have collected money and gifts during our church services, but that these have not found their way to the poor and the oppressed, with the result that the call to practise justice and mercy has been stifled;

(9) that we have given such evidence of misunderstanding and even of slander in our liturgy and teaching that we have dishonoured our neighbour's good name;

(10) that we have let ourselves be deceived in our task in the world by what was in front of us, when we should have given some sign that we had learnt from our liturgy that we should serve the Lord our God, the Father of our Lord Jesus Christ, in faith, hope and love. *Kyrie eleison.*

Translated by David Smith

David Power

Two Expressions of Faith: Worship and Theology

THIS essay is a reflection upon the need to keep the language of theology and the language of worship distinct, but it is at the same time interested in their correlation.[1] By way of introduction, we need to distinguish three things: (a) a spiritual experience, which is grounded in the acceptance of, and commitment to, the meaning of life contained in the Christian revelation; (b) the expression and communication of this experience in symbolic or devotional form, so as to interpret and mediate the experience in a living way, which takes the domain of human feeling into account and enables both community and individuals to relate totally to reality in terms of their faith; (c) the scientific interpretation of the experience and of its symbolic expression, verifying its truth, explaining its presuppositions and categories, achieving some depth of understanding in response to intelligent inquiry.

I. MEDIEVAL THEOLOGY AND DEVOTION

In the twelfth and thirteenth centuries, scholastic and monastic theology sometimes seemed to be at odds with one another. The monks feared a discourse which would turn out to be wholly

[1] The reflection in this article is based principally on the following works: G. Barden, "Modalities of Consciousness", *Philosophical Studies*, XIX (1970), pp. 11–54; M.-D. Chenu, *La Théologie au Douzième Siècle* (Paris, 1957); D. Tracy, *The Achievement of Bernard Lonergan* (New York, 1970), pp. 45-81.

human, a dialectic and a theorizing which would subject the word of God to the tools of human artifice and the reasoning of the human mind, but which would lose contact with the God who spoke through that word. They wanted wisdom, not grammar and philosophy. They sought prayer and contemplation, which would unite with God, not an analysis of human concepts about God. Scholasticism on the other hand dreaded the excesses of allegorism and the sentimentality of an errant piety. It wanted truth, not the wanderings of the human imagination. It believed in a wisdom which could also bring understanding.

This was a problem as old as Christianity, but one which scholasticism tried to approach in a more systematic way and to resolve in its entirety by determining a method of inquiry. Previous centuries had felt and met the need of theoretical explanation of such realities as the incarnation, sin and grace, accordingly as they became matters for concern in the life of the Church, but no system had ever been carefully worked out and applied to the whole body of the Scriptures or of Christian teaching. It was this concern with method which marked the scholastic effort. A Bernard of Clairvaux could be as concerned about the truth as a Hugo of St Victor, an Abelard or an Aquinas, but he did not see the need to submit the whole of Christian truth to a grammar, a dialectic and an analysis.

One however would greatly misunderstand scholasticism if one were to forget the living context out of which it arose. This is as important to scholastic as it was to monastic theology. With monasticism, the scholastics shared the living experience of contemplation and the *vita evangelica*. Indeed, some of them were monks themselves, like the scholars of St Victor—some as noted for their mystic writing as for their systematic expositions. Many of the others had learned to live prayer and evangelism in a new way, as mendicant friars and preachers of the Gospel. Whatever the case, the roots of the great scholastics in the reading and love of the Scriptures, in the experience of prayer and in evangelical brotherhood with all God's creatures is unmistakable. But in the work of theology they had no room for sentiment and the requirements of feeling. There it was a question of the demands of human intelligence and its capacity to understand the word which God had given to men.

One thing which can be usefully noted about scholasticism in our present context is the fact that little enough of its living experience out of which its intellectual inquiry sprang came from the liturgy as then practised. Their world was that of contemplation and gospel brotherhood, of the meditation of the Scriptures as well as of such popular devotions as the crib, the passion of Christ in the way of the cross, the rosary and devotion to the mother of God, or the devotion to Christ present in the eucharistic sacrament reserved. In so far as the liturgy entered into the picture, it was in terms of adapting liturgy to these new trends: providing friars and priests with missals and breviaries which would make daily and private celebration of both Mass and Office possible, the incorporation of new feasts into the liturgical calendar which emphasized devotion to the humanity of Christ, devotion to Mary and devotion to the Blessed Sacrament. It was in these ways and in these exercises that the theologians and men of devotion disposed of themselves to God and entered into the savour of divine wisdom. Many of the elements of good worship are indeed there: Christian brotherhood, the abiding sense of God's presence, devotion to Christ, the Scriptures as life-giving truth, church buildings, church art and devotions of piety which in their own way released the potential and satisfied the need of human feeling and imagination. What may have been lacking is the sense of history, of the momentous importance of the passion and resurrection of Christ as salvific events determining the current of history, and above all the common liturgical action in which all God's people are actively involved, something which provides an experience which in a single symbol system brings all the elements of worship and devotion together.

These comments on the scholastic period are meant to bring out the fact that devotion always remained to be satisfied, even when theory was given such importance. Indeed, without devotion theology is impossible or sterile, a human enterprise and certainly not a divine wisdom. What is also noteworthy is that in the time of which we speak, it was not the liturgy which provided the source of devotion and personal intimacy with God and his Christ, and it is this very lack which made such an excrescence of other devotions necessary.

II. The Complementary Symbolic and Theoretical Expressions of Faith

When we talk of the liturgy as *theologia prima* and distinguish it from another theology, *theologia secunda*, which would be more theoretical and systematic, we are dealing with precisely the same question as is involved in the distinction between the devotional and the theoretical, or between the theory of the scholastics and the living experience which made up their world. It is the same distinction as between the scholastics' savour of God's word and presence and their systematic expositions of theology or between the disposal of themselves to God in contemplation and works and the understanding of the truth which they could objectively affirm in answer to the demands of human reason and the possibilities of human understanding, with all its use of grammar, dialectic, philosophical analysis and logical exposition. It is the difference between communicating intersubjective experience and explaining what that experience is all about.

It can be classed as the distinction between the theoretical and the symbolic, if the symbolic is understood as an affective mode of communicating which allows the human subject to relate totally and to channel all his affective and creative drive into the exchange of persons. The symbolic is concerned with affectivity, it is not detached and disinterested like the scientific mind, it judges everything in relation to the self, it is creative in aesthetic and artistic expression, but also prone to sentimentality and bad taste. It involves the whole person and not just the mind, it looks to feelings rather than directly to understanding. Theory is the opposite to this. Its stress is on disinterested inquiry and understanding, on meeting intellectual demands, answering as far as possible all the questions that can be asked and knowing those which cannot be answered, in evolving methods of inquiry and reflection and exposition so that truth can be as objectively stated as possible and so that new possibilities of inquiry may emerge and be met.

The symbolic and the theoretical are complementary and need one another. This is true of any branch of human living, where vital realities are concerned. It is all the more true in the field of Christian revelation, where ultimate realities are involved. To put it very simply: there must be modes of devotional expression which makes it possible for the Christian person to enter fully and personally into the faith-experience of communion with God, but there must also be modes of theological enterprise which guide the devotional and make intelligent inquiry possible without the hazards of self-interest and sentiment.

How these two enterprises, the theological and the devotional, can interfere with one another, if not kept duly separate, is clear from more than one example. In the absence of a satisfactory worship, doctrinal expression can be made to serve the needs of the affective and symbolic. This is done in more than one way. The most obvious is probably allegorism. A more subtle way occurs when dogmatic formulations are sacralized, turned into symbols which give security in the "faith", presented as something which can be wrapped up in clearly expressed concepts. In such an instance, the sense of being saved through obedience to a system or a formula or an authority substitutes for personal commitment in intersubjective encounter with God. Recent debates about such terms as *transubstantiation* show this ever-present danger, as indeed does the whole controversy of recent decades about catechetical methods and formulations. To grasp this thorny problem with care, it is necessary to advert to the fact that the same formulation sometimes tries to satisfy the needs of both the objective and the subjective. This is particularly true of professions of faith, which are meant to be both the assurance of the objective nature of that in which we believe and also the vehicle for a personal commitment to God in faith. There is no doubt that the profession of faith called the *Apostles' Creed* is couched in symbolic language, that it is concerned with expressing in a kerygmatic way what God and his saving word mean for man. The subtleties of questions about the nature of God and his Christ are absent from its scope, no justification of the presuppositions and foundations of faith is intended. On the other hand, with its formulation of consubstantiality the Nicene Creed has already departed somewhat from the symbolic and the directly salvific to express a concern about objectivity and a more, at least incipient, theoretical expression of the realities involved in faith.

Keeping the distinction between theoretical and symbolic was not made at all easier by the ultimate failure of both the spiritual revival and the theological enterprise which flourished in the age of scholasticism. Unfortunately, the practice of conceptual analysis as an objective in itself dominated theology between Aquinas and the Reform, and the subjective attitude of methodical inquiry was crushed beneath the weight of conceptualism and dialectic practised as an exercise sought for its own sake. Similarly, the living experience of spiritual brotherhood and evangelical poverty were not absorbed into the Church's institutions or liturgy. As the clergy and the faithful grew further apart, the official Church had nothing of the devotional whereby to attract its people or to inspire the theologian to fresh questions. Inasmuch as many of the faithful maintained a concern about the things of God they sought other ways, giving rise to such phenomena as the *fraticelli*, the Hussites or the *devotio moderna*. An institutional Church cut off from a life of piety, a theology likewise cut off from piety, and a piety without a theology to guide it: these were factors which loomed large in creating the disastrous situation of the Reformation era.

After the Reformation and Trent, the living experience of the Catholic Church was one of obedience, fidelity to formulas was the new symbolic which demanded and commandeered affective dedication and personal orientation. It is of course true that the post-Tridentine era contains its own evidence of piety and sanctity, and a living contact with Christ is maintained in such ways as the Ignatian exercises, but it is not with that that we are now concerned. What needs to be pointed out is that very often doctrinal formulation instead of being accepted as the expression of truth and its quest became a symbol of fidelity to the magisterium or the vicar of Christ. Consequently, an apologetic which strove to maintain the *status quo* of the Church's doctrine and institutions replaced theology and permitted no further questions. This attitude influenced liturgy too, for it became a correct procedure, an obedience in rubrics, a way of "preserving the Christian heritage intact", an enterprise which required the right actions and the right words to show submission to God and his representative authority on earth. This is an attitude which still lingers on when a concern with the theological exactitude of prayers dominates concern with the living impact of the words used. Needless to say, this is also bound to end up in a divorce between uncontrolled liturgical experimentation and theology, devoid of a method to deal with such creativity.

The difference between the theoretical and the symbolic is best expressed perhaps when we say that the Christian community needs a language through use of which it can express an objective study and understanding of revelation, and also a language which can incite it to respond intersubjectively to God's call and to dispose of itself to God. It is this latter which ought to be the language of liturgy. The value of the liturgical is its capacity to transmit that Christian experience, deeply felt and demanding, in which God makes his claims upon us. The liturgical movement, in both its official and its experimental expressions, is the focal point of the revival of interest in the Bible as God's spoken word, in spiritual experience, in Christian brotherhood, in a sense of history dominated by the Pasch of Christ, in fellowship with the whole of God's creation, and also the focal point of the difficulty which the Church experiences in coming to terms with these realities and this vision. Liturgy can be the place in which Christian man disposes of himself to God and his fellow man, on condition that it really does serve the need of the symbolic and focuses these elements which have been mentioned.

Theology itself stands to gain from the success of the liturgical endeavour, and in fact needs that success. The new world of living experience which it creates and interprets provides a new stimulus to theological inquiry, a new set of questions to be pondered and a context in which to ponder them. It also provides the spiritual sense which guides the theologian in his work, and the wisdom of union with God which theology shares and tries to formulate. It serves the conversion and the perseverance in the things of the Lord, which must be the mainstay of the theologian's life, which set the norms of his inquiry, the values he holds and the very finality which he pursues.

If liturgy does not provide the Christian community and its

theologians with a conversion-experience in which they commit themselves totally to Christ and to God, in which they sense and experience the presence of Christ and God in the community and the world, they must seek elsewhere to satisfy the desire to taste and see that the Lord is sweet. Or else, bereft of any such experience, theology becomes an arid human process, a new dialectic, a new grammar, a new phenomenology, with little sense of the transcendent. If God at times seems to be left out of current theology, it is perhaps because there is no sense of God, no way or place to savour him. Such theology readily becomes a set of slogans, or a new allegorism, which speaks of brotherhood and liberation, but without much spiritual insight.

On the other hand, theology to be an adequate and objective science needs to develop a method. That was what scholastic theology sought and found, to meet the intellectual demands of its own time and to serve the Church thereby, in a way which would make it possible for it to take account of its own experience and be satisfied that it remained faithful in the pursuit of truth. Some new method is necessary today, as so many of our prominent Christian theologians have realized, with the result that a quest for method is one of the current major preoccupations of theology.

III. The Fundamental Principle of Religious Language

The following quotation summarizes what this essay has tried to say about the need for both the devotional or symbolic mode of language and the theological:

> Now the intention of truth is a dynamism in the subject which is not confined to the symbolic mode but receives its full expansion in the theoretic mode. The unity of the subject and his intentionality indicates the dialectical relation between the theoretic and the symbolic mode; for if the symbolic presentation does not square with the theoretic knowledge then the tension has reached a pitch where the integrity of the subject demands a rejection of one or the other.[2]

[2] Barden, *op. cit.*, p. 54.

This principle which applies to every field of human living is particularly applicable to the religious, where it demands both the distinction and the conformity between the symbolic and the theological.

The theology which is needed is one (a) which makes it possible to certify the truth of what is experienced; (b) which is an examination of the presuppositions and categories of faith, a thematization of the conversion process and an examination of the values and beliefs implied; (c) which is able to distinguish between the symbolic and the doctrinal elements in the profession of faith; (d) which allows for development of the symbolic mode in the community, but can also submit the conversion process and the way in which it is expressed to verification and intelligent inquiry; (e) which is open enough in its formulations not to sacralize them and thus confound the theoretical and the symbolic order.

The devotional on the other hand must not be treated as if it were theology; the purely objective, however correct, is inadequate, for its main concern is subjective participation, not doctrinal accuracy. At the same time, in its devotion, prayer and contemplation the Christian community must have a guarantee that it is constantly in pursuit of God, and this assurance it can obtain from the guidance of a reflective and systematic theology.

PART II
BULLETIN

Mariasusai Dhavamony

Oriental Religions and Worship (a) Hinduism

THE deepest and most persistent aspiration of Hinduism appears to be a relentless quest for the inner experience and realization of the divine.[1] This emphasis on the spiritual realization of the divine in man seems to characterize Hinduism among non-Christian religions. A phenomenological analysis of Hinduism shows clearly that the Hindus have very often responded to the profound aspirations of their religious nature through a variety of religious experiences. Hinduism is known to insist on frequent experience of the divine, inner striving for asceticism and mysticism. It is the strong conviction of the Hindus that all life is the expression of worship, that every act witnesses to the continuous communion of man with God, for they believe that every form of human activity can be turned into the experience and expression of the divine which is immanent in the spiritual self of man. They hold that such religious experience takes place at two levels, corresponding to the material and spiritual nature of man. Hence they distinguish two types of religious experience: empirical[2] and transcendental.[3] We shall describe and analyse both of these in order to bring out their religious significance and to show how they express their faith in them.

[1] I use the word "the divine" in order to include both God (*Iśvara*) of Hindu theists and the Absolute (*Brahman*) of Hindu non-dualists.
[2] "Empirical" in the sense of the experience which is transitory, conditioned by psycho-somatic states.
[3] "Transcendental" in the sense of spiritual experience which transcends time, space and change.

I. Worship of the Divine in Empirical Experience

The empirical religious experience consists mostly of rituals, the practice of virtues, and in general the discipline of action (*karma-yoga*). For Hindus, life in the world, in the social unit and in the individual cannot go on if it is not nourished and stimulated by rites which keep it attuned to the divine. Hindu sacraments are universally practised, for they consecrate the crises and marginal situations in individual and collective life. Prenatal preparations, ceremonies surrounding birth, name-giving, initiation at puberty, marriage, sickness and burial rites are performed by the orthodox Hindus to ward off the dangers lurking in the passage from one stage of life to another and to secure the indispensable contact with the divine source of life. Hindu myths and legends are recited at homes and in public places to create exemplary models of religious life and worship. A significant way through which popular Hinduism expresses its religiousness is to live according to religious myth and ritual. The mythical-ritual way of apprehending ultimate truth becomes a "power unto salvation", a dynamic force whose very embodiment brings forth the sacred reality in everyday existence. In the mythical way of self-realization, the essential structure of the divine manifests itself in particular moments that are remembered and repeated from generation to generation. To live in a myth is to live out the creative power that forms the basis of all existence. The religious purpose of repeating myths and sacraments is not simply to establish a society or to explain the origin of the world but to manifest "what truly is", namely, the sacred.

Worship by means of ritual word (*mantra*) is practised by the rhythmic recitation (*japa*) of certain formulas or words in order to concentrate on the divine nature of the word. The most celebrated ritual word is *oṁ*, considered as the sound-manifestation of the Supreme Being. The entire manifestation of the created order, being names and forms (*nāma-rūpa*), liberation can be obtained by the aid of forms or names[4]: in the case of names,

---

[4] If multiplicity of creation arises from forms and names which are partial manifestations of the divine, then the divine is reached by means of getting hold of the ultimate ground of these manifestations.

they make use of mystical diagrams (*yantra*) which serve as support of meditation, attentive contemplation of which controls or makes cease mental agitation; in the case of forms, the ritual word (*mantra*) provokes by vibrations of sound psychic transformations proper to empty the mind and to leave it pervaded by the presence of the Absolute.

The worship of disinterested service to God is called the discipline of action. The *Bhagavad-gītā* teaches that true worship consists in performing action without being attached to the fruit of action; that it is renunciation *in* action and not renunciation *of* action.[5] The religious man is urged to have, as his unique motive for all action, worship of God with a purified heart. Krishna says: "Do thy work as an offering to me."[6] Work is to be regarded as worship. The man who follows God as his master follows also the Lord's rule and the Lord's rule is to abandon all fruit of work in devotion to him. Thus is acquired meditative calm, full of kindly feeling; for serenity implies an equable mind fostered by calm and steady concentration on the divine. Indifference to the fruit of the action does not mean indifference to the consequences of action. However right an action may be in itself, if it involves loss or injury to others he should not do it. The hallmark of Hindu religious experience is the practice of non-violence, compassion, self-denial and self-giving. If God pervades all, then all must be sacred, and no injury should be caused to any living being. If God is Truth, non-violence is the way to realize him. Gandhi said, "If I were asked to define the Hindu creed, I should simply say, search after Truth through non-violent means." Non-violence is to be adopted not only in one's action but above all in one's thought and attitude towards others. It implies harmlessness in thought, word and deed, as also all-embracing love, boundless and universal. He who has not ceased from immoral conduct cannot obtain God through intelligence. One cannot get to God if one is not "self-restrained", an expression of wide ethical import in Indian spirituality. His belief is that the man of wisdom becomes free of all desires that would hamper his progress towards that supreme knowledge which

[5] 2. 47–48; 3. 19; 4. 19–23; 5. 7–10; 6. 1.
[6] *Bhagavad-gītā* 9. 27.

would loosen for ever all ties and make him one with the Absolute or personal God.

II. WORSHIP OF THE DIVINE IN TRANSCENDENTAL EXPERIENCE

Empirical or moral[7] worship alone, as we have outlined above, is not enough for attaining salvation, although it is quite necessary as a preparatory step. Meditation, knowledge and love are the best means of attaining to the spiritual experience that is central and essential to all genuine worship. Such spiritual acts as meditation, knowledge and love constitute for the Hindus what they call inner worship.[8] The *Upanishads* and the *Bhagavad-gītā* regard meditation and love as internal worship; namely, inner, spiritual realization of the divine which alone belongs to the core of religion, whereas the external act of worship is secondary and valid only in so far as it helps foster the inner.

First, meditation as inner worship of the divine. One has to carefully reflect on the verses of the *Bhagavad-gītā* (Ch. 6–10–32) to learn the art of meditation. What is required of a beginner is ethical purity together with steadfastness of purpose. No difficult postures and no ascetic disciplines are prescribed. One can begin the practice on the lower levels of prayer; he can invoke his chosen deity for success in his enterprise and then pass on to an act of communion with God as indweller in the universe; he concentrates his attention on the immanent God, freed from the interests of his daily life. These two steps are fairly easy. But in the next step of entering the region of the Absolute, God the transcendent, he encounters many obstacles. For hitherto the mind has been functioning as the leader, both in fashioning the prayer on the lips or in the heart in the first stage, and in taking the soul into the depths of the cosmic presence of God in the second. Now it should "abdicate" its function and ultimately efface itself; in this stage all the hidden powers of resistance come to the conscious level; memories of the past, worries of the present and plans for the future bring up from the unconscious unholy or distracting thoughts. Hence the need to rid oneself of these

---

[7] Hindus distinguish morality from spirituality; the former belongs to empirical experience.

[8] *Bhagavad-gītā* 7. 16–19.

and experience the pure subject without object. After prolonged
practice, one will find the mind docile and willing to efface oneself in order to dwell in the Absolute God. It has only to be
perfected by some more practice so that the soul merges into the
Holy of holies. In this connection we have to note that the mind
that is effaced and stilled is very different from what we call
vacant mind. The former is like a bent bow, which at its highest
tension lies silent in the hands of the wielder, while the latter
is like a relaxed bow hung up on a nail in the wall. By the soul
going into its source and consciously experiencing the divine,
the mind grows in the spiritual grasp of the meaning of life,
affording it a deeper and newer penetration into the realities of
ordinary life. This is what the *Upanishads* mean by conquering
death and attaining divine state and consciousness. Steadfast in
meditation, the religious man sees himself in all beings and all
beings in himself—he sees the same in all;[9] that is to say, realiz-
ing the divine he sees all in their source. This produces a sense
of unalloyed peace and happiness; a sense of mystic unity of all
things in the world; it brings about a moral and spiritual revolu-
tion and takes the religious person a step nearer to God.

This higher stage of prayer is called spiritual knowledge
(*jñāna*) by the Hindus. It is a realization of the unity of all things
in God; the multiplicity of things which we see around is only
partial truth. To get at the whole truth we should see not only
the external multiplicity but also the internal unity. In other
words our common sense has to be transcended by mystic sense.
The *Upanishads* declare that he who sees only multiplicity of
things goes from death to death. When a man has a taste of
mystic consciousness and becomes aware of the divine unity be-
hind the multiplicity of things, he naturally longs to remain in
that; it is an experience which destroys all doubt and desire, all
fault and fear, and all sin and sorrow. These mystics not only
live in God and enjoy peace but also are engaged in the happiness
of all beings and are ready to serve their brethren and remove
their suffering. Having partaken of the divine, they are no more
born again; they attain liberation.

Such knowledge of God invariably implies and leads to love

[9] *Ibid.*, 6. 30.

of God. Owing to its intensity, the loving meditation on God acquires the character of an intuitive perception and is exceedingly dear to the soul on account of the supreme lovableness of its object. But this intuitive and loving sense of God does not arise from meditation alone. It is due to the help of grace, a choice gift of God. It requires a total surrender of the devotee to God, for the God of the *Bhagavad-gītā* says, "Love me; on me your mind, to me be your love, for me your sacrifice; to me do reverence; thus truly disciplined and making me your aim, to me shall you come."[10] To win this grace of love, God's help is sought after in a single-minded dedication. Desolate and disconsolate for love of God, Tukārēh prays at his door: "A beggar at thy door, pleading I stand; give me an alms, O God, love from thy loving hand."[11] Some Hindu saints identify God and love; thus Tirumūlar says: "The ignorant say that love and God are two; they do not know that love itself is God. Whoever knows that love itself is God shall rest in love, one with God."[12]

Love of God (*bhakti*) aims at union by love with a personal God. Ordinary or lower experience of love of God is practised by means of rituals, various religious and ascetical observances and the fulfilment of one's duties as marks of one's devotion and love to God. One experiences higher form of love when, going beyond these rituals, injunctions and observances, one experiences directly union with God in love and surrender. Love of God entails the felt participation of the soul in the total being of God rather than the achievement of a transcendental state of bliss. The ultimate realization of this love of God precisely defines a theist mystic's goal. In this experience of union with God the mystic is keenly aware of his total dependence on him and hence he submits himself entirely to the divine action without losing his identity. The *Bhagavad-gītā* assures "By love of God he (the God-lover) comes to know me (God) as I am, he enters me forthwith".[13] Mānikkavācakar exclaims with a profound sense of

---

[10] *Ibid.*, 9. 34.

[11] See Tukārām's hymns in *Temple Bells*, edited by Appasamy (Calcutta, 1958).

[12] For the treatment of Tirumūlar, see my book *Love of God according to Saiva Siddhānta* (Oxford, 1971).

[13] *Bhagavad-gītā* 18. 55.

love, "Thou gavest thyself, thou gained'st me; which did the
better bargain derive? Bliss found I in infinity; but what didst
thou from me derive? My mind thou tookest for thine shrine;
my very body's thine abode; what can I give thee, Lord of
mine?"[14]

III. Conclusion

It is only for the sake of analysis that we separate these various
types of worship and spiritual disciplines (*yoga*) and describe
their proper characteristics. But in actual life they come together
and form aspects of a well-integrated religious worship and practice. Ritual and moral practice lead to inner religious experience
and in the inner experience love and knowledge intermingle,
meditation all along serving as the means of attention and concentration on the divine. In all these types of Hindu worship
the main structure, proper to Hinduism, is a deep sense of the
divine immanence. This spiritual *élan* of the soul towards itself
and towards God finds a favourable climate to receive the salvific action of Christ and thus can contribute to a more profound
Christian experience. We can orientate the Hindu ascetical and
mystical ways of worship towards a sharper and deeper experience of the mystery of Christ. For, in the Hindu experience, we
come across certain values of divine immanence that do not
seem to be accentuated in the Western Christian worship. A
culture that is one-sidedly activistic, exterior and objective tends
to collapse in self-destruction because it lacks the inner depth of
an authentic religious consciousness and no longer experiences
God as other than "dead", with the consequent death of genuine
moral sense, respect for higher values of human life, for to live
without God-consciousness is to live as a beast of burden, carrying one's life with tragic seriousness as a huge and unintelligible
weight. The Hindu tends to fuse action and contemplation in
a fulfilment of religious worship with the specific purpose of
attaining a higher consciousness; namely, consciousness of the
divine immanent presence in the inmost of one's self as the ultimate ground of all existence and to realize union with God in

---

[14] On Māṇikkavācakar see my *Love of God according to Saiva Siddhānta, op. cit.*

love (theist trend) or identity with the Absolute (non-dualist trend) in knowledge. Such inner experience of the divine can surely enrich the Christian worship in the experience and possession of God.

PART III
DOCUMENTATION
CONCILIUM

Herman Schmidt

Faith and its Confession in an A-religious World

IN THE last ten years or so, the number of books and articles written about prayer has grown enormously[1] and I have had to make a ruthless selection. In the first section of this documentation, I have concentrated on a number of aspects relating to Christian faith in the modern world—credibility and truthfulness and incredibility and untruthfulness, the faith of intellectual Christians, faith in literature and resistance and conversion from below. In the second section, I discuss the most important publications and collected works dealing with modern confessions of faith and, in the third section, some publications about the experience of faith.

I. CHRISTIAN FAITH IN THE MODERN WORLD

The refined yet degenerate Graeco-Roman world of the early Church was in many ways not unlike our own. Christ chose Paul to be the apostle of the Gentiles, in other words, of the people or pagan nations. Helped by special charismatic gifts, Paul not only brought Christianity as *leaven* to the centres of culture of his own times—Corinth, Galatia, Ephesus, Philippi, Colossae, Thessalonica, Athens and Rome—but was also able to overcome the initial lack of understanding of this hitherto unknown situation

---

[1] See Herman Schmidt, *Bidden onderweg van 1960 tot 1970; Documentaire studie met bibliografie en citaten-selectie* (Haarlem, 1971)—this work includes 642 titles; *Wie betet der heutige Mensch? Dokumente und Analysen* (Freiburg, 1972)—this work contains 1221 titles.

prevalent among the Jews in Jerusalem. The Acts of the Apostles is therefore, together with Paul's letters, especially relevant to our own period.

There is, however, a real difference—Paul brought faith to non-Christians (*non-credentes*), whereas the modern Church has the task of bringing faith to unbelievers (*infideles*) who have turned their backs on Christianity. This is also the case to some extent even in Asia and Africa, where the Church proclaims the Christian faith among unbelievers from the West who bear the name of Christians. There is no need to define the situation of Christianity in the modern world in this article—it has already been sufficiently discussed elsewhere.

1. *Credibility and Truthfulness—Incredibility and Untruthfulness*

All the churches are keenly aware of the need to renew their thinking and to go back to the one source of faith, Jesus Christ himself. The World Council of Churches was set up precisely in order to overcome the scandal of division and the Second Vatican Council set afoot a process of profound renewal. But, as in the past, this work is hindered because of the protective attitude of the official representatives of the churches towards their positions of power and their determination to cling to antiquated legal and theological systems.

One good example of this is the liturgy in the Roman Catholic Church. The renewal of the liturgy, as the source and climax of the life of faith, is a positive achievement, yet the negative aspect of this is also apparent in the determined defence of the specifically Catholic way of life as expressed in the liturgy and the inability or refusal to understand that being a Catholic today, celebrating the liturgy, means conversion and commitment.

The result of this is that the Church has come to be regarded as incredible and untruthful. Too little has so far been written about this pressing problem of incredibility and untruthfulness, although its painful effects on the life of faith are well known.

Hans Küng has written a book on truthfulness which is perhaps too emotional and aggressive—*Wahrhaftigkeit; Zur Zukunft der Kirche* (Freiburg, 1968). Wilhelm Gössmann's book, *Glaubwürdigkeit im Sprachgebrauch; Stilkritische und Sprachdidaktische Untersuchungen* (Munich, 1970), is a sober and objective analysis of credibility in the use of language. Gössmann is a specialist in the science of religious language and has also written sample prayers; his works are of considerable importance to liturgical specialists. Gotthold Hasenhüttl has written an essay about a credible community in the future: "Eine glaubwürdige Gemeinde der Zukunft", in O. Betz (ed.), *Gemeinde von morgen* (Munich, 1969), pp. 175–186. Johannes Lehmann has published several essays dealing with the question of credibility and incredibility and of the "sickness" of faith; see especially *Ist der Glaube krank? Glaubwürdigkeit und Unglaubwürdigkeit der Gläubigen* (Stuttgart, 1966). Finally, the question has frequently been discussed incidentally in many books and articles.

The consequences of this incredibility are clear enough. Many Christians lose their faith while others continue to call themselves Christians, but break all links with the Church, with the result that they become fringe members of the Church. The majority of Christians who remain loyal despite their experience of incredibility *within* the Church are strengthened by this purification of their Christian lives in their faith in the credibility and truthfulness *of* the Church, the Body of Christ, who is always with his Church in spite of the faithlessness and even betrayal of its members.

2. What have Christian Intellectuals to say about Faith?

A number of books have been published giving the answers made by intellectuals to questions about the attitude to revelation and faith.

H. Schultz has written a book about piety in a secular world: *Frömmigkeit in einer weltlichen Welt* (Stuttgart, 2nd edn., 1959), in which people from various walks in life speak positively about faith and in which the problems of, the opportunities facing and the initiatives open to Christianity are discussed. José Gironella has interviewed a hundred well-known Spaniards about their attitude to God in *100 Españoles y Dios* (Barcelona, 4th edn., 1969)—their reactions vary from extremely positive to extremely negative. Answers to the question: "Who is Jesus Christ for you?" have been published in *Pour vous qui est Jésus-Christ?* (Paris, 1970), with similar extremes of positive and negative. An inquiry into the faith of young teachers has been published in the journal *Christus*, 17 (1970), pp. 488–572. Finally, all sociological surveys of the religious life provide interesting data.

The most interesting aspect of these publications is perhaps that, in addition to a majority of really convinced Christian testimonies, there are many answers which reveal quite a superficial or conventional life of faith. The reactions of unbelievers compel the Church to an examination of conscience What has above all to be borne in mind is that, in all these publications, it is intellectuals who are expressing their faith or lack of it.

3. *Faith and Literature*

Most modern literature is either completely a-religious or else less interested in religious problems and the phenomenon of faith and lack of faith. Here, I can do no more than mention a representative selection.

(a) Domenico Porzio has chosen passages from the writings of 203 internationally known authors during the last hundred years describing encounters and collisions with Christ in his *Incontri e scontri col Cristo* (Milan, 1971). His book was very well reviewed and stimulated Paul VI to make contact with a number of writers (see *Osservatore Romano*, 29 January 1972), to speak to them about his own encounter with Christ and to give them his book *Cristo nell'uomo d'oggi*.

(b) The standard work on this subject is Charles Moeller's *Littérature du XXe siècle et christianisme* (Tournai), in which the author surveys Christianity in twentieth-century literature. Four volumes have so far been published. Moeller's *L'homme moderne devant le Salut* (Paris, 1965) has received awards and has been translated into several languages.

(c) There have been many good publications, some containing contributions by different authors, on faith and literature, including some with a liturgical emphasis: H. Beckmann, ed., *Godot oder Hiob; Glaubensfragen in der modernen Literatur*

(Hamburg, 1965); W. Grenzmann, *Dichtung und Glaube*; *Probleme und Gestalten der deutschen Gegenwartsliteratur* (Bonn, 5th edn., 1967); G. Hierzenberger, ed., *Unterwegs zum Menschen; Texte und Kommentare zum Selbst-, Welt- und Gottesverständnis in der Literatur des 20. Jahrhunderts; Zum Gebrauch an der Oberstufe des Gymnasiums* (Munich, 1970)—this publication includes a textbook and a workbook; *Moderne Literatur und christlicher Glaube* (Munich, 2nd edn., 1969).

(d) Giuseppe Berto has written a play about "the passion according to ourselves", *La Passione secondo noi stessi; Un atto preceduto da un prologo* (Milan, 1972); the action of this play takes place in a restaurant in one part of which Jesus' contemporaries appear and in the other part men of today, including a psychologist and a sociologist; Christ's suffering is discussed and faith and unbelief collide with each other.

(e) A mixture of faith and unbelief and of many different religions will be found in the following works: Wassilij Rosanow, *Gedanken aus dem Hinterhalt; Ein Katechismus für Ketzer* (Zürich, 1971)—this book is translated from the Russian; Otto Spachtholz, *Poesien aus religiöser Innenschau mit einstimmenden Akkorden in Prosa; Religion aus Leben und Dichtung; Gott, Tao, Brahma; Ein Betrachtungsbuch für Menschen aller Bekenntnisse* (Vienna, 1971); Theo Govaart, *De vele beelden van God; Van Tao Te King tot G.K. van het Reve* ('s-Hertogenbosch and Antwerp, n.d.), in which the author presents many different images of God; "Raam op Religie", *Raam Literair Maandblad*, 82 (1972), in which several Dutch writers write about their religious views.

In the above selection, I have mentioned only a few publications out of a vast number in which faith and unbelief are discussed most explicitly. Specialists in liturgy, catechetics, theology and pastoral work must make themselves familiar with modern literature in order to know and understand the ideas and attitudes of the people for whom they are working. Even more important than a knowledge of literature as such, however, is a familiarity with what is happening in the sphere of mass entertainment—stage, music, film, radio and television—which exerts such an enormous influence on contemporary man. It would, however, be impossible to include this within the present documentation.

4. *Resistance and Conversion from Below*

My main preoccupation here is, of course, with what is being done as it were from above, that is, in intellectual circles, to help the spread of Christian faith in the modern world. It is, however, important not to overlook entirely the spontaneous reactions of young people especially against the often alarming developments that are taking place in society, although very little literature as such is available. Young people are neither pessimistic nor optimistic, but tend to be realists and are often so striking in the way in which they express themselves, very often outside the official churches, that they have for a long time attracted the attention of the world press. Countless groups appear spontaneously, disappear and appear again. Now we have the Jesus movement and pentecostalism. What will it be next year? The enormous number of songs and musicals about Jesus and the Spirit certainly shows that these are at the moment "in". Groups of young people are not simply *talking about faith*—they are *believing* and *being converted* and their *way of life* is their resistance to contemporary society. It is easy enough to criticize this "realism" from the sociological point of view, but more difficult to do *realistically* what these young people are doing unrealistically.

It is necessary to make this rather brief comment because I am in the main concerned here with what intellectuals who are no longer so young are doing and this inevitably gives rise to such questions as what is the real significance of the Church's official and semi-official work for the younger generation? Do young people still listen to the Church? Is the Church's language really unintelligible to young people? Have they written the Church off as irrelevant? What meaning has the life of faith as expressed by the Church and, for example, the renewed liturgy for the rising generation? Do young people today refuse to accept an *institution* and *authority* or is it more true, perhaps, to say that they reject concrete institutional forms and the concrete exercise of authority and may go so far as to behave anarchically towards real or supposed moral power imposed from above? In such cases, it is clearly better not to speak about faith or to celebrate the liturgy. Religion is no longer the opium of the people now that flight from reality is made possible by easily obtainable drugs of all kinds. Faith and liturgical celebration must be experienced *now* as something of value to those who are above all concerned for the *future*.

II. Modern Confessions of Faith

Liturgists, catechists, theologians and pastoral workers in the West are especially preoccupied nowadays with the need to find an intelligible and up-to-date confession of faith, while continuing to use the traditional formulations (the *Symbolum Apostolicum* and the *Symbolum Nicaeno-Constantinopolitanum*) in their original form, in an adapted version or as criteria for new confessions. The scientific editions of the confession of faith in the many different forms in which it existed in the early Christian communities provide clear proof that it is not only in the twentieth century that this need has been felt.[2]

Two new formulations have been officially promulgated in the Roman Catholic Church since Vatican II. The first is basically the Nicene Creed with a short introduction and a new ending.[3] This is intended to replace the Tridentine formula and the antimodernist oath, both of which had, according to canon law, to be made publicly and subscribed to in certain cases. The second is a confession of faith solemnly pronounced by Paul VI.[4] This closely resembles a new draft confession of faith composed by the preparatory commission of theologians for the Second Vatican Council, but not dealt with by the conciliar fathers.

As Wolfgang Beinert correctly said, "It is clear that the question 'old or new confessions of faith' is a wrong one. There can be no question of doing away with the early creeds and composing modern ones and the polemics conducted by those who support the 'old' formulas against the supporters of the 'new' are bound to be sterile. In the community of believers, only one thing is of importance—that faith and love are lived as they were in the early Church which tried to give them living expres-

[2] See, for example, F. Kattenbusch, *Das Apostolische Symbol; seine Entstehung, sein geschichtlicher Sinn, seine Stellung* (Leipzig, 1894–1900), two volumes; J. Kelly, *Early Christian Creeds* (London, 2nd edn., 1960).
[3] *AAS*, 59 (1967), p. 1058.   [4] *AAS*, 60 (1968), pp. 436–45.

sion in its formulations. We must try to do the same today, perhaps in 'old', perhaps in 'new' words. All that matters is that it really takes place."[5]

1. *Collections*

There is a great deal of interest among theologians in Germany in this whole question and a number of collections of new texts, drawn from a variety of German and foreign publications, have been published there. This interest in new confessions of faith began as long ago as 1934, when the Federation of German Evangelical Confessing Churches declared its opposition to Nazi tendencies among Christians at Barmen. From 1945 onwards, this attitude has come to be expressed principally as a criticism of existing confessions of faith, both from the creative and from the theological point of view. Increasing interest has been taken by Roman Catholic theologians in the formulation of confessions of faith.

(a) Hans Steubing has published texts of confessions of faith spanning a period of twenty centuries and including many non-Roman Catholic confessions since the Middle Ages in his *Bekenntnisse der Kirche; Bekenntnistexte aus zwanzig Jahrhunderte* (Wuppertal, 1970). Most of the texts in Gerhard Ruhbach's *Glaubensbekenntnisse für unsere Zeit* (Gütersloh, 1971) originated in local German Evangelical churches. Gerhard Ruhbach, Henning Schröer and Manfred Wichelhaus have provided a great deal of material drawn from the Evangelical churches together with detailed criticism and analysis in *Bekenntnisin Bewegung; Ein Informations- und Diskussionsbuch* (Göttingen, 1969). An ecumenical collection of texts with introductions and commentaries will be found in Josef Schulte's *Glaube elementar; Versuche einer Kurzformel des Christlichen* (Essen, 1971). The most comprehensive collection of Roman Catholic confessions of faith has been made by Roman Bleistein in his detailed critical study *Kurzformel des Glaubens* (Würzburg, 1971), two volumes. These collections are especially valuable because the material is drawn from such a great variety of sources.

[5] W. Beinert, "Die alten Glaubensbekenntnisse und die neuen Kurzformeln", *Internationale Katholische Zeitschrift*, 1 (1972), p. 114.

(b) Dutch Protestants have also shown an interest in this question. Eimert Pruim has compiled a rather haphazard collection of forty-nine texts originating in Holland and abroad and in different churches in a booklet of twenty-three pages without sources or commentary: *Credo's onderweg; Nieuwe woorden voor God, wereld en Kerk* (Delft, 1971). M.P. van Dijk has provided a new confession of faith together with a commentary for the Dutch Calvinist-Zwinglian Reformed Churches in his *Nieuw Credo; Proeve van een nieuwe belijdenis* (Kampen, 1970). This sample creed has the following structure: Of the Father and our creation, Of the Son and our redemption, Of the Spirit and our renewal, Of Holy Scripture, Of the sacraments, Of the commandments, Of prayer.

What is most striking about the German texts is the use of the term *Kurzformel* or "short, abbreviated formula", apparently first employed by theologians who were attempting to express the essential aspect of faith in the fewest possible words. Karl Rahner achieved a certain fame with his "short formulas" and Roman Bleistein[6] quotes his three drafts, the first of 1964 being six and a half pages long, while the second and the third of 1969 and 1970 respectively consist of only one page each and are divided into theological, sociological and futurological formulas. Alex Stock has commented in detail on the Christian content of Rahner's second draft formula.[7] Both Bleistein's and Stock's books contain good bibliographies and Josef Schulte includes four attempts to make Rahner's first draft intelligible to non-theologians.[8]

Other theologians who have followed Rahner in an attempt to express their teaching in a "short formula" include F. Varillon, H. Schuster, W. Nastainczyk, W. Kasper, R. Bleistein and H. Küng.[9] The creeds of the Dutch theologians P. Schoonenberg and P. Smulders will be found in Pruim's collection.[10]

---

[6] R. Bleistein, *Kurzformel des Glaubens* (Würzburg, 1971), II, pp. 86–94.
[7] A. Stock, *Kurzformeln des Glaubens; Zur Unterscheidung des Christlichen bei Karl Rahner* (Zürich, 1971).
[8] J. Schulte, ed., *Glaube elementar* (Essen, 1971), pp. 99–100, 110–12, 115–16.
[9] R. Bleistein, *Kurzformel des Glaubens, op. cit.*, II, pp. 94–102.
[10] E. Pruim, ed., *Credo's onderweg* (Delft, 1971), pp. 14, 19.

These short theological formulas, of course, only indirectly influence the expression of faith in the liturgy and in catechetics and pastoral work, which is inevitably much more varied. In addition to Bleistein's book, Hanno Keller's study of the recent development of confessions of faith is important in this context.[11] Liturgical, catechetical and pastoral confessions are extremely diverse. Some abbreviate, revise or paraphrase the Apostles' Creed. They may be trinitarian or they may simply be directed towards the Father, the Son or the Spirit. They may express the subjective faith of an individual or of a group, in which case they are probably more sociological and futurological. Most take man living in the modern world as their point of departure and aim to arouse him to the reality of love and to redeem him from sin and isolation. The authors of these free liturgical, catechetical and pastoral confessions of faith do not try to do something that it has never been possible to do even in the classic Apostles' and Nicene Creeds, that is, to express the whole content of faith in a "short formula". What is more, no attempt is made now in these spheres of Christian activity to limit the confession of faith to a single formula. On the contrary, modern man is expected to express his faith in many different ways according to the changing situations in his constantly developing environment. He is not, moreover, looking necessarily for an abstract or theoretical *science* of faith, an orthodoxy, but for a way of expressing a richly varied *life* of faith, an orthopraxis, in the community of believers.

Both orthodoxy and orthopraxis have to be subject to the critical norms of each period in history and each society. Faith may, for example, be "corrected" if the Apostles' Creed is shortened by the omission of the word *unicum* referring to God's Son or of *virgine* in connection with Mary. The difficult art of translating ancient texts has also to be understood—an example of this in the Nicene Creed being the word *consubstantialem*.[12]

---

[11] H. Keller, "Bekenntnisbildung in der Gegenwart", G. Ruhbach, H. Schröer and M. Wichelhaus, *Bekenntnis in Bewegung* (Göttingen, 1969), pp. 162–213.

[12] See, for example,, E. Nida, *Toward a Science of Translating; With Special Reference to Principles and Procedures Involved in Bible Translating* (Leyden, 1964).

Both of these creeds are works of art and are therefore a legitimate source of inspiration for free adaptations and simplified versions in different languages in later periods and societies.

One free version of the confession of faith that has aroused a good deal of discussion in recent years is the so-called "Political Night Prayer" of Dorothee Sölle,[13] whose theology is now very well known.[14] Many critics have tended to reject this confession of faith and M. Haug, for example, has even questioned whether it can really be regarded as Christian.[15] Dorothee Sölle denies the transcendence of God and sees the world as closed in on itself, confessing the death of God in brilliant language: "I believe in Jesus Christ who is resurrected in our lives. . . ."

2. Writings about the Confession of Faith

Very many works have been written in the last few years about the confession of faith. Those mentioned below are mainly intended to confirm and deepen the life of believers.

(a) The following publications provide a great deal of information and good bibliographies. Wolfgang Beinert has written an article which forms a useful introduction to the modern problem confronting the ancient confessions of faith and to the new "short formulas": "Die alten Glaubensbekenntnisse und die neuen Kurzformeln", *Internationale Katholische Zeitschrift*, 1 (1972), pp. 97–114. Attempts to compose a "short formula" of faith have been described in *Herder Korrespondenz*, 23/1 (1969), pp. 32–8, in an article entitled "Bemühungen um eine 'Kurzformel' des Glaubens". K. Lehmann has made notes on and a bibliography of contemporary "short formulas" in "Zum Problem einer Konzentration der Glaubensaussagen", *Lebendiges Zeugnis*, 3–4 (1970), pp. 15–44, also in 'Kurzformeln des christlichen Glaubens", in B. Dreher, N. Greinacher and F. Klostermann (eds.), *Handbuch der Verkündigung* (Freiburg, 1970), I, pp. 274–95.

[13] D. Sölle and F. Steffensky, *Politisches Nachtgebet in Köln* (Stuttgart and Mainz, 1969), pp. 26–7.
[14] D. Sölle, *Atheistisch an Gott glauben; Beiträge zur Theologie* (Olten and Freiburg, 4th edn., 1970).
[15] M. Haug, *Ist das Glaubensbekenntnis von Frau Dr. Sölle noch ein christliches Bekenntnis?* (Stuttgart, 2nd edn., 1969).

G. Schneider provides information about the problem of the reduction of theological statements in "Zur Problematik der Reduktion theologischer Aussagen", *Catholica*, 25 (1971), pp. 179–97.

(b) Two theological essays on the *Symbolum Apostolicum* and the *Symbolum Nicaeno-Constantinopolitanum* are relevant to this question. Henri Bouillard has written a very striking essay on the name of God in the Creed, "Le nom de Dieu dans le Credo", in the acts of the 1969 annual symposium of humanist and philosophical studies at Rome, edited by E. Castelli and published under the title of *L'analyse du langage théologique; le nom de Dieu; Actes du colloque organisé par le centre international d'études humanistes et par l'institut d'études philosophiques de Rome* (Rome, 5–11 January 1969; Paris, 1969). The whole of this book is of importance to our theme. The second essay is by P. Smulders, who has investigated "Some Riddles in the Apostles' Creed" in *Bijdragen*, 31 (1970), pp. 234–60 and 32 (1971), pp. 350–66.

(c) The ecumenical German translations of the Apostles' and the Nicene Creeds have been discussed in W. Beinert, K. Hoffmann and H. von Schade, *Glaubensbekenntnis und Gotteslob in der Kirche; Apostolisches und Nizänisches Glaubensbekenntnis, Gloria, Sanctus, Agnus Dei, Gloria Patri; eine Handreichung zu den ökumenischen Neuübersetzungen* (Freiburg, 1971)—a book which would serve as a model for anyone who is concerned with the translation of liturgical texts today. H. Moeuvres has written a commentary on the Creed used at Mass in *Visage de notre foi; le Credo de la Messe* (Paris, 1971).

(d) I list below some of the many commentaries on the Apostles' and the Nicene Creeds intended for non-specialist readers. In German: V. Hahn and M. Kratz have published addresses in *Ich glaube und bekenne; Ansprachen zum Apostolischen Glaubensbekenntnis* (Limburg, n.d.). A lively and easily read report of dialogues about faith and confessions of faith has been published by Eberhard Müller, *Gespräch über den Glauben; Informationen über die Bedeutung der christlichen Glaubenssätze* (Hamburg, 1963). J. Ratzinger's lectures about the Creed are well known even outside the German-speaking countries: *Einführung in das Christentum; Vorlesungen über das Apostolische Glaubensbekenntnis* (Munich, 1968) and Henning Schröer's book on the confession of faith today is, in my opinion, especially valuable: *Unser Glaubensbekenntnis heute; Versuch einer theologischen Bilanz* (Hamburg, 1971). It is hardly necessary to recommend H. Thielicke's excellent book on the "confession of Christians", *Ich glaube; das Bekenntnis der Christen* (Freiburg, 1971).

In French: Henri de Lubac's essay on the structure of the Apostles' Creed is outstanding—*La foi chrétienne; Essai sur la structure du Symbole des Apôtres* (Paris, 1969). In Italian: Alessandro Pronzato has written a book containing a text from world literature on the theme of the Christian creed for every day of the year—*Io credo; Giorno per giorno* (Turin, 1969).

In Dutch: E. Henau has published twelve articles on the creed in *Ons geloof; Begrijpen en artikuleren* (Antwerp, 1969).

(e) Those who have been baptized in the Dutch Reformed Church are confirmed at the end of puberty and made active members of the community of the Church in the unity of the Holy Spirit. Those who do not accept this confirmation are not regarded as active members and not admitted to the Lord's Supper. The confession of faith plays a very important part in this confirmation and there have consequently been many books published about the creed intended for young people. A few of these, in my view the most typical, are listed below. A. Barkey Wolf has written three books—*Dit bidden wij ... dit belijden wij; de kern van ons geloof* (Zwolle, n.d.); *Tongen als van vuur; Gedachten over het betekenisvolle woordje "Als"* (Zwolle, 1963) and *Tussen moeras en luchtspiegeling* (Zwolle, 1962). The word "yes" is emphasized in two different publications—G. Luchtigheid, ed., *Ons JA tot GOD; een boek voor de jonge Kerk* (Zwolle, n.d.) and in a collection of essays, *Het grote "Ja"; een boek voor de jonge Kerk* (Zwolle, n.d.). C. van der Wal has stressed the importance of the words "amen" and "to give consent to" (in Dutch to "say amen to") in *Amen en beamen: Doop, belijdenis, avondmaal* (Kampen, 1971).

Almost all of the books and articles that I have listed above are in the main intended for use in the liturgical, catechetical and pastoral spheres. Like all human communities, Christians have their own experiences, their own language and their own means of expression. Christian education is essential because the modern Christian lives without protection in an a-Christian environment and the Church's language must above all be biblical and its actions sacramental and liturgical. Rationalistic and scholastic concepts in theology are no longer understood in the modern world. The churches can no longer rely on systems of thought which were effective in the Middle Ages and at the time of Luther and Calvin, but which are no longer acceptable in a democratic and scientifically orientated society in which everyone has the opportunity of education and is open to the influence of the mass media. So long as believers know that Scripture and the sacraments are not scientific systems or mechanical actions, but values which never become antiquated, a return to them will not be a flight into the ghetto. However difficult it may be to interpret Scripture and to make sacramental actions meaningful to modern man, it is both possible and necessary to do so, because Christian language and action must preserve an element which is uniquely and distinctively Christian. The gift of faith enables the Christian to speak and to act differently from the atheist and the strength of his faith is that he believes in *someone* rather than in something. His faith is not another ideology alongside other ideologies, but above all a personal surrender to, a being possessed by a personal God, the Father, the Son and the Holy Spirit. The Christian finds his special language and his special way of acting in these personal relationships.

This is the background to the modern interest in confessing, celebrating and living faith. A Protestant author has said, in one of the many publications that I have read, that, despite the central importance of Scripture in the Protestant churches, the formula of the confession of faith is even more important. It would not be wrong to say that the traditional view in the Roman Catholic Church is that teaching about faith is more important than anything else. The churches, however, are gradually dissociating themselves from these attitudes and are beginning to regard the Word of God and the activity of the Spirit of Christ as of primary importance and the formulas of faith and teaching about faith as subordinate to these. Christians are freeing themselves from the attitude that Alexander Schweizer (1808–1888) expressed in an aphorism: "Our fathers confessed their faith and we take great pains to believe their confessions."[16]

Finally, Christian confessions of faith must always contain some distinctive element which will attract the attention of those who are outside Christianity as such. Helmut Gollwitzer has put it in this way: "Confessions of faith which do not result in profound social changes are merely private pleasures and are therefore tolerated as irrelevant and harmless."[17]

III. The Experience of Faith

To conclude this documentation on faith and its confession in an a-religious world, I should like to draw attention to a number of publications dealing with the experience of faith. Since the liturgy is now celebrated in the language of the people, man's experience of the mystery of faith can be developed completely from the psychological point of view, perhaps even to the point where a balance can be achieved between the content and the experience of faith. At the same time, it is clear from the ever-growing number of books and articles written about prayer in the widest sense that the subjective aspect of this experience is receiving much more attention. Of course, the word "experience" has so many shades of meaning—it is not a clear concept. Unfortunately, I have not come across any analytical or historical study which attempts to define it. The following works are by authors bearing witness to their own experience of faith and prayer.

It is to some extent an "experience" to listen to monks "experienced" in prayer and the liturgy and continuing to "experience" God in their lives—a typical experience can be gained from reading "Attention à Dieu et expériences de prière; Le colloque monastique d'Orval, septembre 1970", in

---

[16] This quotation from Schweizer, who was a pupil of Schleiermacher's, is taken from H. Schröer, *Unser Glaubensbekenntnis heute* (Hamburg, 1971), p. 17.

[17] See G. Ruhbach, H. Schröer and M. Wichelhaus, *Bekenntnis in Bewegung* (Göttingen, 1969), p. 232.

Collectanea Cisterciensia, 33 (1971), pp. 3–128. A. Louf has written an interesting book on becoming aware of God through learning how to pray—*Heer, leer ons bidden; Iets gewaar worden van God* (Tielt and Utrecht, 1971). M. Noël's book *Erfahrungen mit Gott* (Mainz, n.d.) is also worth reading. Jörg Zink undoubtedly understands how Scripture should be brought to the people so that it can be a contemporary experience for them—*Die Wahrheit lässt sich finden; Dokumente aus der Bibel und Erfahrungen von heute* (Stuttgart, 2nd edn., 1972).

Ideas about "experience" will also be found in J. Bours, *Gott erfahren?* (Munich, 1971); I. Hermann, "Glauben und erfahren", in O. Betz, ed., *Gemeinde von morgen* (Munich, 1969), pp. 187–200; see also *Gotteserfahrung und Gottesverlust* (Graz, 1966), published by the Catechetical Institute of Graz University.

Although I have been prevented by reasons of space from quoting from a selection of the very many new confessions and prayers of faith in this documentation, I should like to conclude with one concrete example of a modern creed. It is the creed of Cardinal Giulio Bevilacqua (1881–1965), who was at one time parish priest of the parish of S. Antonio at Brescia.[18]

I believe in God
and I believe in man
 as the image of God.
I believe in men
 in their thinking
 in their exhausting work
 which has made them to be what they are.
I believe in life
 as joy and as tenacity:
 not a short-term loan threatened by death
 but a gift with a purpose.
I believe in life
 as an unlimited possibility
 of elevation and sublimation.

[18] Published in M. Tosco and L. Rosadoni, eds., *Autori vari: Salmi dell'uomo d'oggi* (Turin, 1971), pp. 97–8.

I believe in joy;
the joy of every season
    of every stopping place
    of every dawn
    of every sunset
    of every face
    of every ray of light
        which comes from the mind
           from the senses
           from the heart.

I believe in the possibility of a great human family
    as Christ wishes it;
    an exchange of all the achievements of the spirit
    and of all hands in peace.

I believe in myself
    in the ability that God has bestowed on me
    because I can experience the greatest of all joys—
    that of giving and of giving myself.

Translated by David Smith

Biographical Notes

IRÉNÉE-HENRI DALMAIS, O.P., was born in 1914 in Vienne (France) and ordained in 1945. He studied at the Saulchoir, at the University of Lyons and at the Sorbonne. He holds degrees in literature, philosophy and theology and has been professor of Oriental liturgy at the Higher Institute of Liturgy in Paris since 1956. Among his published works are: *Initiation à la Liturgie* (Paris, 1958) and *Saints et Sanctuaires d'Orient* (Paris, 1968).

MARIASUSAI DHAVAMONY, S.J., was ordained in Kurseong (India) in 1958 and is professor of Hinduism and of the history of religions at the Gregorian University, Rome. He is a licentiate in theology, doctor of philosophy of the Gregorian University and doctor of philosophy (Oriental religions) of Oxford University. He is editor of *Studia Missionalia* and *Documenta Missionalia* and has written many books and articles.

LANGDON GILKEY was born in Chicago in 1919. He studied in the United States at Harvard College, at Columbia University and at the Union Theological Seminary. Doctor of philosophy, he has been reader in religion at Vassar College and professor of theology at Vanderbilt Divinity School of Nashville, Tennessee. In 1963 he became professor of theology at the University of Chicago. In 1965 he received a Guggenheim prize to enable him to study Catholic theology in Rome. Among his published works are: *Maker of Heaven and Earth* (New York, 1959), *How the Church can Minister to the World without Losing Itself* (New York, 1964), *Shantung Compound* (New York, 1966), *Naming the Whirlwind: The Renewal of God-Language* (New York, 1969) and *Religion and the Scientific Future* (New York, 1970). He has also written articles on providence in contemporary theology, the social and intellectual sources of contemporary Protestant theology, etc.

CASPER HONDERS was born in 1923 in Holland. He studied theology in Holland (Gröningen, Leyden and Amsterdam) and Switzerland (Basle and Zürich). From 1951 to 1963 he was a pastor in the Reformed Dutch Church. He gained a doctorate of theology at Amsterdam in 1963. He has published books on the history of the Church, on liturgical science—notably an edition of the text of the *Liturgia Sacra* (1551–55) of Valerandus Pollanus—and on Church music, particularly the works of Johann Sebastian Bach. Since 1963 he has been attached to the Institute of Liturgy of the University of Gröningen and is a member of the editorial committee of the International Fellowship for Research in Hymnology.

JEAN LADRIÈRE was born in 1921 in Nivelles (Belgium). He studied philosophy and mathematics at Louvain University. Licentiate in mathematical sciences, doctor of philosophy, he has been *professeur ordinaire* at Louvain University since 1959. Among his published works are: *Les limitations internes des formalismes* (Paris and Louvain, 1957) and *L'articulation du sens* (Paris, 1970). He has contributed many articles to different philosophical reviews, notably the *Revue Philosophique de Louvain*.

GERARD LUKKEN was born in 1933 in The Hague. He studied theology and liturgy at the Major Seminary of Haaren (Holland), at the Gregorian University (Rome) and at the Institute of Liturgy (Paris). Doctor of theology, he is reader at the Faculty of Theology of Tilburg. He has written a number of articles, mainly for *Liturgisch Woordenboek, Questions Liturgiques* and *Tijdschrift voor Liturgie*.

JEAN-PIERRE MANIGNE, o.p., was born in 1935 in Paris and was ordained in 1966. He studied at the Faculties of Theology of the Saulchoir. Licentiate in philosophy, licentiate and reader in theology, he is a contributor to *Informations Catholiques Internationales*. He is the author of *Pour une Poétique de la Foi* and of "Le sens du Poéme" in *Revue des Sciences Philosophiques et Théologiques*.

DAVID POWER, o.m.i., was born in 1932 in Dublin and ordained in 1956. He studied at the St Anselm Institute of Liturgy, Rome. Licentiate in philosophy and doctor of theology, he is professor of sacramental theology at the Gregorian University, Rome. Among his published works is *Ministers of Christ and His Church* (London, 1969).

HERMAN SCHMIDT, s.j., was born in 1912 in Roermond and ordained in 1940. He studied at the University of Nijmegen and in Rome at the Oriental Institute, the Institute of Archaeology, the Institute of Sacred Music and at the School of Palaeography of the Vatican. Licentiate in philosophy and doctor of theology, he is professor of liturgy at the Gregorian University and at the St Anselm Institute of Liturgy, Rome. Among his published works are: *Introductio in Liturgiam Occidentalem* (Rome, 1965³) and *Constitutie over de H. Liturgie* (Antwerp, 1964).

BRUCE VAWTER, c.m., was born in 1921 in Fort Worth (Texas), joined the Lazarist Fathers and was ordained in 1947. He studied at the University of St Thomas and the Pontifical Biblical Institute, Rome. Doctor of Sacred Scripture, he is now professor and president of the Department of Theology at De Paul University, Chicago. Among his published works are: *A Path through Genesis, The Bible in the Church, The Conscience of Israel, New Paths through the Bible* and *Biblical Inspiration*. He has contributed numerous articles on exegetical studies to scientific reviews, including *The Catholic Biblical Quarterly* and *Journal of Biblical Literature*.

EVANGELISTA VILLANOVA, O.S.B., was born in 1927 in Rubí (Spain) and ordained in 1952. He studied at the St Anselm Athenaeum (Rome) and the Institut Catholique (Paris). Doctor of theology, he is professor of dogmatic theology at the Faculty of Theology of Barcelona. He is also editor of the review *Questions de vida cristiana*. Among his published works are: "Vías históricas de la autoreflexión de la Iglesia" in *Comentario eclesial a la Ecclesiam Suam* (Bilbao, 1964), "Cinquanta anys de teologia de la liturgia" in *Il Congrés litúrgic de Montserrat* (1965), and, his last work, *El magisteri eclesiàtic en l'ensenyament de la teologia* (Barcelona).